MIDDLE CLASS SUPPORT

A Route to Socioeconomic Security

BOOKS BY ROBERT THEOBALD

The Rich and the Poor (1960)
The Challenge of Abundance (1961)
Profit Potential in the Developing Countries (1962)
Free Men and Free Markets (1963)
Business Potential in the European Common Market (1963)
The Guaranteed Income, ed. (1966)
Social Policies for America in the Seventies, ed. (1968)
An Alternative Future for America II (1970)
Bobbs-Merrill Dialogue Series, ed.
Teg's 1994 (1972)
Habit and Habitat (1972)
Futures Conditional (1972)
Economizing Abundance (1972)

MIDDLE CLASS SUPPORT

A Route to Socioeconomic Security

edited by
Robert Theobald

Second Revised Edition

THE **SWALLOW PRESS** INC.
CHICAGO

Copyright © 1968, 1969, 1972 by Robert Theobald
All rights reserved
Printed in the United States of America

Second revised edition
    First printing 1972

Published by
The Swallow Press Incorporated
1139 South Wabash Avenue
Chicago, Illinois 60605

This book is printed on 100% recycled paper

ISBN 0-8040-0612-1
Library of Congress Catalog Card Number 72-91921

This book was originally published as *Committed Spending* by Doubleday & Company, Inc. in 1968 and by Anchor Books in 1969

CONTENTS

Introduction to the Second Edition   ix

Preface   xxxvi

THE IMMINENT REVOLUTION IN
CYBERNATION
   Irving E. Kaplan   1

SECOND-ORDER COMMITTED SPENDING:
THE SUPPORT OF INNOVATION
   R. Christian Anderson   30

EFFECT ON ARTISTIC ACTIVITY
   George Nelson   47

TAX IMPLICATIONS
   Kendall P. Cochran   65

SOME SOCIAL CONSEQUENCES OF
A GUARANTEED INCOME
   Margaret Mead   93

CONTINUING EDUCATION AND BASIC
ECONOMIC SECURITY
   A. A. Liveright   117

MANDATE FOR LEARNING
   Don Benson   139

THE CHALLENGE OF ECONOMIC
SECURITY TO RELIGION
   Henry Malcolm   164

AFTERWORD: THE LONG-RUN RESULTS OF
A DESIGN FOR ECONOMIC SECURITY
   Robert Theobald   186

APPENDIX: THE DESIGN FOR ECONOMIC
SECURITY AS ORIGINALLY PUBLISHED
IN *FREE MEN AND FREE MARKETS*
   Robert Theobald   196

CONTRIBUTORS

R. CHRISTIAN ANDERSON is assistant director of Brookhaven National Laboratory. His interests include pure science as well as the impact of new scientific knowledge on society and the ways in which society can be best organized to ensure intelligent development of further knowledge. He is a member of various learned societies and has participated in international conferences on science and society.

DON BENSON, editor of *Dialogue on Poverty*, attended Massachusetts public schools, Norwich University, Amherst College, Goddard College, and Southern Illinois University. He has worked with the Vermont Department of Education, the University of the Streets in New York City, and the Friends World College.

KENDALL P. COCHRAN has been professor of economics at North Texas State University since 1957 and previously taught at Ohio State University and the University of Texas. He is a member of the executive committee of the Association for Evolutionary Economics and a director of the National Science Foundation Economics Institute. He is the author of numerous reviews, articles, and papers.

IRVING E. KAPLAN is a consulting psychologist in the San Diego area. He first began to forecast the appearance of new technology and its implications for work, culture, and human values in 1960 while serving as a researcher and research program director for the Navy. His numerous research reports have been read widely within the United States, Great Britain and Canada.

A. A. LIVERIGHT was director of the Center for the Study of Liberal Education for Adults at Boston University, Professor of Education at Boston University, and secretary of the International Congress of University Adult Education. He served as a consultant and wrote widely in the field of adult education. He has died since this work was originally published.

HENRY MALCOLM is Protestant counselor and Presbyterian university pastor at Columbia University. His ministry comprises an application of psychoanalytic theory and practice together with a radical Christian approach to individual and social pathology.

MARGARET MEAD is curator of ethnology at the American Museum of Natural History and adjunct professor of anthropology at Columbia University. She is a specialist in various areas including education and culture and the relationship between character structure and social forms. She has written widely about the culture of both the United States and other nations as well as of isolated tribes.

GEORGE NELSON has his own office for architectural design. He has worked on corporate identity programs, designed exhibitions, products, interiors and exteriors for homes, factories, and offices as well as graphics. He also holds teaching appointments at Yale, Columbia, and Pratt Institutes.

ROBERT THEOBALD is an India-born socioeconomist who, since 1957, has been studying the effects of abundance on the American socioeconomy. In recent years he has been primarily concerned to develop methods of informing people about the implications of the new technologies.

INTRODUCTION TO SECOND EDITION

This book is concerned with the minimal, immediate steps which must be taken if we are to prevent the development of a permanent dispossessed class in the United States and the other rich countries of the world. This dispossessed class will have two parts. First, there will be those who never rose out of poverty or left the slums. Second, there will be those who will lose their well paying jobs as the effects of automation and cybernation — with their requirements for far greater efficiency — begin to be fully felt.

The developing split between the possessed and the dispossessed is profoundly different in nature from the threefold split of the industrial era — i.e., the split between the rich, the middle-class, and the poor. During the industrial era, differences in income levels were great, but they did not prevent people from seeing themselves as all being part of the same society. People believed that they — or their children — could reasonably expect to move upward in the society.

Today, there is already a semi-permanent dispossessed underclass which lives in ways very different from those of the possessed. The possessed are respectable, they are very well-off in historical terms, and they have access to credit and credit cards. The dispossessed, usually those without jobs, have neither adequate monetary resources nor access to credit. Those who drop out from the possessed into the dispossessed rapidly lose their credit-worthiness and also their access to the information resources required to keep themselves up-to-date and skilled. They therefore often fall rapidly into a permanent place among the dispossessed.

The fall-out of people from the possessed to the dispossessed is more rapid than we care to admit — or the unemployment statistics reflect. Further, we disguise the nature of the process which is taking place by keeping people in college at the beginning of their lives and by "early retirement" when they are old. The following editorial, reprinted from *Product Engineering*, throws light on some aspects of the unemployment statistics issue.

[In the winter of 1970] a spokesman for the Engineers Joint Council calculated unemployment among engineers as 3.7%, using data from the Bureau of Labor Statistics. At the same time he cited a recent Engineering Manpower Commission study indicating that in 1971 unemployment among aerospace engineers would be in excess of 25%.

Recently we published a BLS report that engineering unemployment is now "up to 3%" — a report to which many engineers would take strong exception.

In the aerospace industry, employment is down nearly 30% from its previous peak. In the largest companies it is down even more. There are not any realistic data that we have been able to find on the proportion of these unemployed in aerospace who are engineers, but that 25% prediction from the Engineering Manpower Commission looks rather conservative.

When the Numerical Control Society held its annual meeting in California [recently] there was a good deal of comment among the members about the problems of the 15-member organizing committee from the Los Angeles chapter responsible for the meeting. All but a couple had "changed jobs" during the period while the meeting program was being planned. Some were still "temporary consultants" at the time of the meeting.

Engineering employment in the aerospace industry has been harder hit than anywhere else, but there have also been substantial reductions in automobile, electronic, and other industries.

Our reporters in Washington have been trying to isolate the reasons for the gap between what the BLS says and what we see. The BLS data are based on an area probability sample of 50,000 families. The employed are those in the sample who worked for pay for at least one hour in the reporting week; the unemployed are those who were actively looking for work in the past four weeks, unless they are on layoff or have a new job that will start within 30 days.

The accuracy of the data is dependent on the memory and understanding of the family members who answer the question. Engineers represent less than 2% of the employed, and this makes some people question the validity of the sample, though there is substantial evidence that the samples are carefully chosen, statistically reasonable, and accurately tabulated. They should give a fair picture of the total number employed.

But there is another reason why the results are not accurate for professional occupations. If an unemployed engineer takes a temporary job for two weeks as a taxi driver replacing a regular driver who is on vacation, the engineer will then be classified not as an "unemployed engineer" but as an "unemployed taxi driver." If he takes a permanent job as a taxi driver, the engineer ceases statistically to be either unemployed or an engineer.

According to the BLS, the number of engineers increased by 28,000 from 1968 to 1969, then declined by 19,000 in 1970. Graduations from college took place at about the same level as before, and the difference between +28,000 and −19,000 could well represent 47,000 engineers who gave up on their profession in 1970.

You must also remember that the official average unemployment of engineers was 0.7% in 1968 and that when it recently hit an official 3.0%, that was an increase of more than 300% in the number of unemployed engineers. That kind of increase makes quite a difference in the problems of job seekers.

Some of these paradoxes in government statistics have been embarrassing the Nixon Administration lately. The answers of technicians in the BLS to the questions asked at the regular press briefings have not always squared with the optimistic statements coming from the Secretary's office and the White House.

The solution to this problem on the part of the Administration has been to discontinue the press briefings. We don't think efforts to conceal the size of the problem solve anything. They only serve to weaken confidence in all government statistics.

Data are cold and hard, however. They fail to reflect the personal tragedies which occur as well-educated, imaginative people are deprived of opportunities to use their skills. The following two stories show some of the consequences. Keith Bose is a technical writer who lost his job in 1970. Many months later he finally found a job — but one that fails to use his real potential. This article was written while Bose was seeking re-employment.

I am unemployed. I am not part of an ethnic minority. My great-grandfather voted for Abraham Lincoln and wore union blue. I am part of an increasing number of so-called middle-class unemployed who are now viewing the splendor of the nation's economy from its soft underbelly. Our numbers will increase in this new decade. We are only the vanguard of future legions as 20,000,000 more workers reach an adult working age in the next 10 years.

Many of Richard Nixon's silent majority are discovering that only the thickness of a regular paycheck separates middle America from the slum. In our preoccupation with the superfluous glitter of the affluent society, we have failed to discover that true affluence must be backed by ownership.

Middle America does not hold title to its affluence. We are not true bourgeois, for we are unpropertied. We buy precarious status on time payments. Our chattels become worn out and obsolete when title passes to us. Our "affluent" consumer economy is a vast parasite feeding on our earnings, and neither frugality nor industry will help us escape.

There is a creeping sensation of futility that follows the white-collar worker to his job these days — a feeling of being an expendable pawn in an economic system that does not, in fact, include human service in the tenuous fiction of the Gross National Product. The white-collar worker suffers from a pitiful lack of bargaining power. If black America is crying for recognition, white middle America is praying that the myth of indispensability will endure.

Behind the facade of white stability lurks the haunting realization that the economy has a tragic surplus of white-collar workers.

It is finally becoming possible to garner bland statistics to support facts that the middle American has felt in his bones for a long while — that more and more workers are becoming surplus and, therefore, fall under the control of Parkinson's law: Trivial, superfluous work expands as more and more people become available to do it.

Those who want to understand middle America must understand that the maintenance of uninterrupted regular wages is mandatory to our existence.

If we appear uninterested in the politics of government, it is because we are consumed by the politics of keeping our job.

An unemployed, middle-aged former head of an electronics-firm department tells it this way:

"At 4:30 on Friday I was called into the conference room. Charlie and Phil were sitting there with a small pile of papers. I sat down. My hands were sweaty.

"Charlie began the conversation. 'As you know, business is off. We are going to have to terminate you, effective today....'

"I didn't have any witnesses with me, and they had each other covered. They gave me papers to sign. I asked to be allowed to take them home first to look them over.

"Phil said, 'You will have to sign them now so we can clear you by 5 o'clock.'

"And that's how it was. After 25 years — the bastards terminated me in 15 minutes."

For those who would garner a middle-class constituency, remember that the psychological pressure on us is soul-destroying. Soon in our careers we trade ethical and professional judgment for a regular salary. We were compromised. Buried in the trivia of our 'career,' we drifted without protection along a debt-ridden path to nowhere. For many of us, outstanding skill and moral judgment were a hindrance.

There is a satisfying notion that employment is related to education. We have been told that any number of jobs are available if only persons with education and experience could be found to fill them. For many of the unemployed and underemployed, these assumptions have become a cruel hoax. The honest need for mechanical, electronic, and other specialists was met long ago.

Some sections of the United States have been shocked by unemployment in the aerospace industry. We had forgotten that government-sponsored industry sparked earlier growth.

World War II and Korea thrust manufacturing into the peaceful potato fields. During the '40s and '50s, military aircraft poured from runways. But as the 1960s dawned, large-scale production of military hardware faded. To get contracts, firms doing business with the government pushed for glamor products framed in the mystique of "systems design," which featured large proportions of engineering personnel with fewer blue-collar production types.

On the surface it would appear that the "defense worker" is well paid for trivial work, hence more fortunate than those burdened by the competition of a free marketplace. Unfortunately, the defense worker was not as well off as it seemed even before the current extensive cutbacks. Many jobs in Pentagon-sponsored work do not exist in ordinary commercial enterprises. Once a worker accepts this line of endeavor, he is doomed forever to depend upon the vagaries of Pentagon contracting.

A few days ago, one unemployed systems engineer, sitting in his tastefully furnished living room, exploded, "The aerospace industry is middle-class welfare in disguise!" These are bitter words, and many would like to dismiss them as sour grapes.

But it would be interesting for someone to examine the curious process whereby millions of middle-class Americans are able to find a job in the first palce. Examination of the "help wanted" section finds many exotic specialties. A recent newspaper lists:

Manpower development specialist.
Production traffic analyst.
Quality assurance supervisor.
Logistic control engineer.
Financial aide.
Planning analyst.

All these positions stipulate graduate degrees coupled with ponderously described past experience. Sometimes these jobs disappear when business sags — a process that appears in the financial pages as "trimming the fat." Few businesses are immune from fat-trimmings. Edward Booher, a vice president at McGraw-Hill, told the New

York Times:

"We've reduced our staff 5 percent across the board, or about 250 people, since last fall. . . . I wouldn't say it was just because of the recession. We've grown so fast we found that we had to stop for a while and start eliminating some duplicate functions."

In such a way we describe 250 human tragedies. Now there are 250 souls adrift among the statistics, none of whom can become "manpower development specialists," "planning analysts," or God knows what because a vast, coercive mechanism has been erected that is weighted heavily toward the employer with jobs to offer.

A familiar psychological ploy is to capture the loyalty of the mediocre professional by paying him far more than he can earn anywhere else. This ancient technique is always good for a faithful slave. It is a characteristic of Pentagon-sponsored firms, since the government picks up salary tabs. Yet it is dangerous to assume that unemployed professional workers are dolts who may be neglected by politicians.

When mass layoffs hit Long Island about a year ago, a few of us knew that we would have to help ourselves by working together.

"We formed a little group called Self Help," Fred Thome, 50, said. "I got over the shock of being laid off and decided to do something. When Self Help was formed, I volunteered for the action committee. It is time for us Americans to stop boondoggling and start thinking of the future . . . of our children and their children. In 75 years the world will run out of fossil fuel. We are riding our 250-horse-power, chrome-trimmed chariots to destruction."

Figures presented by the shamans of the Bureau of Labor Statistics are being called a fraud by members of Self Help, who spend time when not job-hunting doing research in employment figures. One unemployed engineer has discovered that 67,000 engineers have disappeared from the government count over the last year.

"When an engineer becomes a taxi driver and gets laid off, he is no longer an engineer but an unemployed taxi driver, according to the government," he said. "I never had much confidence in bureaucracy, but now I am losing confidence in government itself."

Employment in Pentagon-sponsored industry is down by 30 per cent. It does not seem possible for this many specialists to have found re-employment in the depressed civilian economy. It would be more logical to assume that these men are unemployed or partially employed and have disappeared from the population count of the Bureau of Labor Statistics.

The key to middle America is silence. When Richard Nixon pandered to his silent majority, we responded with the smug assumption that we were silent out of inherent dignity. Now we are unemployed, and we are agonizing with introspection. Richard Nixon insulted us by calling attention to our silence. Did he know that we were silent out of laziness, stupidity, and fear?

Laziness is unpleasant to admit. We have basked in the fiction that Americans are ambitious. But for the hundreds of thousands of middle-aged men now unemployed, we cannot look back upon evidence of ambition.

Our adult lives began when we were drafted for military service. The furor of the media over Vietnam hides the fact that the life of an American serviceman is easy by international standards and disgracefully few soldiers ever really fight.

After brief military service, as new adults we became eligible for subsidized college attendance under the GI Bill. College during the '50s was more an exercise in conformity than an intellectual experience. That was the beginning of our stupidity, in the days of the organization men who passed psychological tests and believed that the world cried for their services in vague contributions that still remain undefined. That was the decade when 2,400,000 of us accepted "professional" and technical jobs.

Professional life for us became an exercise in trivia, relieved only by the pleasures of split-level materialism. Buried in a job characterized more by jargon than the discipline of honest technology, we took little interest in politics and we are baffled by the political gimmickry of today's campus.

But millions more workers have come of age, and gradually, over the last decade, competition for jobs has grown vicious. At some point in the life of every idealist comes the discovery that the virtuous worker is not necessarily rewarded. There was probably a time in a pristine economic order when lower-level workers could find a small measure of security simply by doing their job. Today craftsmanship and excellence are nostalgic relics.

As the economy exploded during the 1950s, garrulous young personnel officers circulated pleasant rules for management-employee relations. The cult of "professionalism" guaranteed civil and amenable relationships. It was, by and large, a happy time for middle America. Now much has changed. We were seduced by the glittering marketplace, and now we have been left alone and helpless to contemplate the birth of the bastard conceived in a drunken liaison when we fancied ourselves a legitimate part of the relentless economic power structure that now mocks us.

Few of us read well and our ability to communicate in written English is a travesty, highlighting the fraudulent educational process that produced us. Aside from the elusive requirements of our daily tasks, we have added nothing to our knowledge that cannot be presented on a 19-inch screen.

Vaguely we realized that we had no trade skills in the accepted sense. At some point in our careers we became conscious that we had no profession at all, and we hungered for a secret jargon to protect us, as hippies devise secret words.

Our burgeoning suburban neighborhoods are unlike the immigrant neighborhoods of an earlier day, whence we allegedly came. We lack the organization of family ties, parishes, and clubs of those early days and cannot even call upon the paternalism of a local political boss when circumstances crush us. We men haven't even the good sense to congregate in a corner bar to exchange homely wisdom.

In our ignorance we are castigating Nixon. The smart money knows that. Since Democrats come cheap, voting majorities will cost less in 1972, barring inflationary trends. Now the Democrats can trot the image of good old F.D.R. out to the suburbs.

Being unemployed forces us to become amateur politicians and economists. In the pursuit of this new interest, we unemployed people know that credit manipulation and federal reserve currency maneuvers are a long way from producing jobs in an economy that will be joined by 20,000,000 new workers in the next 10 years. Black Muslims are closer to reality when they propound the religious tenet that the United States never will be able to furnish enough jobs for the millions of white unemployed, let alone 20,000,000 blacks.

We have described our laziness and stupidity, but what about fear? Imagine us in our black horn-rims, clad in wrinkled Bond suit, clutching our briefcase of miserable trivia, hurrying through our bureaucratic halls. What do we fear? Maybe it is our own ignorance.

By now my plaintive theme should emerge: The tragic issue of the United States is not even being debated.

The population of the country has increased by 26,000,000 in the last 10 years. Each day industry learns to produce more by using fewer persons in honest work. The pressure is being felt throughout the working force. Nothing in economic theory will give these surplus citizens power to bargain in the marketplace for their existence as human beings, let alone defend constitutional rights. We are coolies, hiding in the tinsel of suburbia.

The largest, most powerful institutions of the United States are those that minister to our surplus population. That explains the enormous growth of colleges and our military establishment. The inherent characteristic of any military establishment is that it provides the means of occupying the services of legions of men.

Looking back on my life so far, I am impressed with the tragic waste of human potential in our system, and this is a terrifying paradox.

From Marx to Keynes, the assumption has been that the intelligent and educated always will find their services of value in the human marketplace. This notion is reaching an ignominious end. When we focus on the bare skeleton of any economic scheme of things, we must admit that compensation for useful labor is a classic form of legally recognized distribution of money to the populace. The system is breaking down because we have contrived a socioeconomic system that denies the vast bulk of society the right to perform economically useful services.

Maybe it is time for us to redefine work — and then get back to work.

The second personal story is from a welfare recipient who, for reasons made obvious in her article, has requested that she not be identified. The article is reprinted from *City* magazine.

In April, 1971, I was laid off from work; by November, 1971, I am still out of work. For me, this period of my life has been one of learning — but not book learning.

While working, I was constantly running into people who not only complained about welfare rolls but also condemned welfare recipients. Perhaps *condemned* seems like too strong a word, but believe me that is what a recipient feels like when they hear people talk about us as being "content to be on welfare" or "lazy," "having a free ride," etc.

While I could expect those who have no personal experience with poverty to not know any better, I have been constantly amazed to hear these stereotype condemnations come from those who do have experience. The most extreme example of this is a girl (known to both myself and my cousin) who had been a welfare recipient for several years. Somehow her caseworker got on her and made her go to work. After she had been working for about two months we ran into her on the street one day. After the usual hellos were said, she started talking about how welfare recipients could get jobs if they wanted to, how welfare recipients were lazy, etc. And, dig it, she had only been off the rolls two months herself and only went to work after extreme pressure — threats to cut her off. What made it so bad was, we remembered her referring to her caseworker as all kinds of "motha's" when he first started leaning on her. Not only that, she bitched about "What was the matter with him anyway? You'd think the money was coming out of his own pocket!"

Now I don't know if she had gone through the process of selective forgetting or not. But after running into her, I began to think about people's reactions to me when they heard or hear I'm on welfare. When I mention it after they ask what I am doing, their eyes start to take on a glazed look and they start moving on very quickly. You'd think I said I had VD instead.

What seems to be more striking is that these "fast

movers" are not the so-called black bourgeoisie of whom this behavior is said to be typical; the fast movers are former co-workers or colleagues in community action programs. You know the type. The people — many with college degrees — who boast about their offices being in the "inner city" and who refer to neighborhood inhabitants as "the folks"; who are very quick on the freedom handshake and say "Hello brother" or "Hey sister" to every black person they pass on the street out of an attempt to show how "real" they are.

On my better days I try to understand these unreal fast movers by understanding or trying to understand that they are all in programs that are ultimately and basically controlled by Chuck — no matter how many black faces they got running around the administrative and board-of-directors end of things. Chuckie controls the purse strings and anytime he feels like yanking them he can. And when and if he does, all my former colleagues are gonna be right in the welfare line with me. (If not all, a hell of a lot.) By realizing this, I figure that maybe when they see me, they realize just what can happen to them. And nobody likes to face the unpleasant side of reality.

I'm not ego-tripping either. I have two college degrees, and a lot of experience both job- and volunteer-wise as a social-psychological researcher, sensitivity trainer (in both personal and institutionalized racism encounter groups), on-the-street community organizer, etc. I've been at this before the gravy train started rolling — for 12 years. So like, when I have trouble getting a job, folks know that times is hard.

I have run into black Ph.Ds in the unemployment office, and, believe, it was my turn to be shocked! A lot of these brothers got caught in the aerospace and engineering cutbacks. And when we looked in the employment book, the engineering jobs were very specifically defined: 15 or 10 years' experience might be asked for. Now really, how many brothers have 10 to 15 years in engineering?

And dig, these "brothers" felt smug about not being on welfare. Why? Because in unemployment they were only getting back what they put in. They weren't living off what they hadn't earned. So then I asked just where in the hell did they think welfare money came from? If they had paid taxes, then where was the stigma since a lot of their taxes went to pay welfare. And so on and so forth.

What makes these views of people on welfare puzzling is that they come from people who support efforts to cut down the workweek, but still receive the same salary they are getting now. It's all very strange. But what is even stranger is what we on welfare and/or unemployment find when we try to get off the rolls. But before I get into that, a word about getting on the dole is in order.

I went on welfare as a result of going to the unemployment office and finding that I couldn't collect compensation under the laws of my state (Pennsylvania). No one can who works for a nonprofit organization, a teacher, a nurse — even state employees. However, I was encouraged to register with the unemployment job section so that they could help me get a job.

In the meantime, since I was really in a tight I decided I should go to the welfare office. It was noted that once I had worked in another state and maybe I could collect from it. However, it would take time for this to come through, if at all. Since I was down to my last five, off to the welfare office I went.

At the welfare office I was given an appointment for another day on which I would be seen by an intake interviewer. And I could not get any emergency money to tide me over until I had seen her. When I returned I was to bring a complete dossier of my financial standing — bank account, stocks, bonds, mortgage, lease, etc. For me this was easy, I only had a lease to bring in.

It was in the intake interview section where I really learned new lessons — although the learning process was begun at the unemployment office. The chief lesson was that both agencies do not really exist to help a person, while they may represent themselves as doing so. To me, to help means to assist or aid in overcoming a situation. In my experience, welfare and unemployment exist to either maintain a person in bottom-of-the-barrel city poverty or to bring the person into it.

For example, the rent for my slum area apartment is $140 a month. And note that I had been living in it for more than a year before I went to the welfare office. At the intake interview, I was told that I would have to move.

Why? Because the monthly allotment for a single person in Pennsylvania is $123. The $123 is to cover everything: rent, clothes, groceries (food stamps also), transportation. And dig, while told I would have to move, it was also pointed out that not only was it too bad that I would have to go to worse conditions but welfare would not and does not pay the moving bill out of the $123. It was at this point I decided that if my out-of-state unemployment claim came through, I was going to keep it and not tell welfare anything about it. And I didn't give a shit if it was and is illegal.

I pointed out that I had job interview appointments out of state which could be verified. Would welfare provide carfare at least? I could brown-bag something to eat. Answer: No. The appointments would have to be kept out of the allotment I received — $123. Needless to add, I had to cancel some of the appointments. Others I kept by borrowing money. No, I didn't get the jobs.

The reasons given of course were the usual: either overqualified or, while qualified in say four out of five areas, the missing fifth was the really important one. But I frequently wonder if the fact that I was appearing at these interviews with glasses on that had one lens cracked in three places and the frame held together with cement glue helped.

The intake interviewer gave me a welfare medical card and told me I could get my glasses fixed with it. However, the clinic stated that they would not and could not take me without a letter from my caseworker. I did not have a caseworker. Too bad, they said. I received no aid from the medical assistance bureau of the welfare department. When I called a doctor in the neighborhood, I was told that he was only permitted to take children on welfare. In order for him to take me, I would have to join the Bureau of Vocational Rehabilitation, get a letter from them that gave him permission to treat me.

Of course, unemployment doesn't really help a person get a job either. Financially, the only money a person gets is their weekly allotment. And I suppose what's fair is fare (sic). But this is how they work:

Once signed or registered, a person is urged to come in every morning to look at the job books. If you find a job you would like to try for, you then fill out a card, hand it in, and wait for an interviewer to call you. No, you can't just go out to the place. The job books do not list the address or company of the prospective employer. Only the job interviewers have it.

Once called, the interviewer makes sure you have understood the requirement correctly. Then, to save you a trip, the interviewer calls the company to find out if the job is still open. If it is, they relate the relevant background of the job seeker over the phone. If everything is still okay, then they give you the company and address. Sound fair? Maybe. The only problem is, if you get hired, you or the company are supposed to notify the unemployment office. If this happens, you are immediately taken off the rolls.

Unless a person has some savings somewhere, this can cause a problem. With the new job, the person now has the expenses of transportation to and from the job, lunch, and possibly new clothes or having the old ones cleaned. These have to be paid for between the time of the stopping of the unemployment checks and the starting of the payroll checks. Since unemployment money is money a person has accumulated, it would seem fair to let the person, on request, continue to collect until a paycheck shows up. Remember, in starting a new job, a person can wait six weeks sometimes before the first check. I suppose it is possible to ask for an advance. But that really scores goody points with the boss, doesn't it? There you are, first day on the job, asking for a handout.

At one point, I decided to pursue something I had always felt a person, no matter how educated, should do: Learn a good solid trade. Reason: A good solid trade is always employable.

In looking at the job books, I saw a job for a trainee. The employer would pay you while you learned. So I filled out the card and took it to a job interviewer. She pointed out that the trainee slot paid less than I was getting on unemployment. Being fair and all, I agreed and then pointed out that once I learned the trade, I'd be set. Then she agreed. I didn't like her agreement and thought it over. Then I asked the big question: Since the trainee spot paid less than I was making, wouldn't I continue to receive at least a portion of *my* unemployment money to make up the difference? Answer: No. Now, it is true that with the unemployment I was (illegally) collecting welfare, but I still was barely able to "make it." So a cut in my take would be really a hassle. I could really look forward to having a hole in my sole. What could I do? She wouldn't tell me where the place was so I could go on my own and maybe get the job and not tell her. There was not much of a choice. I had to let it go.

At this point, I wonder how many of you agree that welfare and unemployment do not really help a person get a job. Not only that, the unemployment office misleads you into thinking there are more jobs available than there really are. When I really learned to read the numbers that surround the job descriptions, I found that a large number of the so-called available jobs have been in the books so long that whoever got it is probably collecting retirement pay.

After being caught over and over again in binds like these described, I wonder how people expect us to keep looking for work. And yet, many of us surreptitiously do so. Perhaps because our efforts to do so are undercover and thus not listed as a statistic, people are really unaware and continue to assume that we are "content."

While the description above about trying to get a job is accurate, it could use some filling out. The picture of trying to get a job on welfare is not complete, nor is the picture re unemployment.

Some people can get more on welfare than from any job they could get. Then why do they work? Part of the reason is to keep from going crazy. Vacations are one thing, but permanent vacations are murder. If not, then why is it that so many people who are forced to retire decline rapidly physically, psychologically, and emotionally? And take it from me you do.

Since I have been out of work, I've been physically ill every time I looked around — mainly colds with temperatures. Not only that, I've had things I've had at no other time in my life — e.g., a badly sprained back and a torn cartilage in the knee; also a cold in the nerves of my other leg. Coincidental? I don't know. But I find it interesting that the only time I have ever had a problem with my limbs was a sprained ankle when I was 17 — 14 years ago.

I used to get deliberately bombed or stoned by noon so I wouldn't have to face the fact that there were too many hours of daylight left and I had nothing to do. A unique frustration. Nowhere to go and nothing to do and even if I had something to do — no money to do it with.

In being on poverty now, a person really learns what it is like to lead a life of "quiet desperation." Add to the frustration the rage and outrage of having your life to a high degree controlled by the systems on which you are dependent. If you attempt to be completely honest with them, then you come as I did to feel at the mercy of anyone who wants to fuck you over. Once this feeling gets through, a sort of mental checking goes on. A result of this is to discriminate between being fucked over by the system or by your friends. A sort of détente is reached inside of your being. It wasn't until I had "preached the funeral" of one or two friends and relatives that I realized that my insides had decided to be cool around the systems, but Lord help anybody else.

And there comes a time or a limit at which I and other clients and recipients draw the line. I can't define the time or the limit, but it seems to work in this way: In being poor or becoming poor, I reached an undefined state in which I no longer asked for or sought help in meeting certain needs. It is as though the worse off I got, to ask for something would no longer be requesting, it would be begging.

For example, while I was still trying to look for a job, the phone company notified me that it was going to cut off my phone. When job hunting, a phone is your lifeline. On receiving your resumés, companies don't write back, they call. This notice came when I was up to the proverbial "here" with asking for jobs. I was also up to here with attempts to get my needs met through the system. I did absolutely nothing about the phone. It got paid because a friend tried to call me, found the phone disconnected, and went and paid the bill. She (Pat) did so without saying anything to me. She later told me she knew I needed the phone, but there was no way in life I would have taken the money if she had offered it to me. I had reached my limit.

It takes a lot of energy to be poor. It takes a lot of energy to have to go and beg for assistance to survive. It takes a lot of energy to keep occupied so that you don't have time to think about the condition we're in. It takes a lot of energy to not think that tomorrow means the same as today — nothing. It takes energy to find a little job where the boss won't report your salary. On unemployment, a person can earn a certain percentage of what they collect and still keep what they collect. But if that percentage is exceeded, no check. It takes energy when there is no food in the house and your food stamps have not arrived, to go find out what happened. It takes energy to not kill your caseworker who made an appointment with you and keeps you waiting a couple of hours — who then sends another person to tell you that if you can wait maybe three more hours he'll be available. It takes energy to not let your rage out but inside of you like a time bomb. It takes energy to believe that some of these programs that are supposed to aid the poor really will. It takes even more energy to not feel like a fool when they really don't.

I go to bed eagerly desirous of sleep and wake up in the morning more tired frequently than when I was working. I don't think I really have to explain why.

How can we expect the dispossessed to react as their numbers increase with the impact of automation and cybernation? Will the dispossessed unite to demand a new way of distributing rights to resources? Or will some of those who lose their jobs feel that they should not be caught up with the dispossessed — that their displacement results from social injustice and political ineptitude rather than from the realities of technological change?

The next article, written by Walter Goodman in *The New Leader*, implies that we shall not necessarily move toward an understanding of the real forces at work. There could well be a movement backward to old values and past life-styles rather than an attempt to discover the new patterns required by man's increasing power.

On a visit to Southern California a few weeks ago, I spent a morning with a 38-year-old electrical engineer — call him Frank White — who had been laid off from his $14,000-a-year job with North American Aircraft in

April 1970, when the firm completed its work on the Apollo project. In November, having gone through his unemployment insurance, his vacation pay, and his modest savings, and having borrowed the maximum on his life insurance policy, he applied for welfare. His years of steady employment had given him a breathing space of just seven months. Since November, he has been supporting his wife and three young daughters with a combination of welfare payments and odd jobs.

Frank's predicament is not uncommon today in distressed centers of the aerospace industry, from Orange County to Long Island. He had been laid off from jobs before, but "then, when one company was coming down, another was coming up. It's a high-pay, high-risk industry. Only this time they're all down. It's happened everywhere." He has sent out about 100 resumés in the last year, and keeps the regretful refusals in a looseleaf book along with other mementos.

Obviously, it is most disagreeable to have to be concerned over losing one's house — Frank has so far managed to cover the mortgage payments, but doesn't know how he's going to meet his real estate taxes when they fall due; to have to let one's bills slide until the dunning letters become seriously threatening — "the utilities don't fool around, they'll cut off the electricity"; to accept an occasional loan from a relative with no prospect of being able to repay it; to stop buying clothes and going to the movies; to eat more macaroni and cheese than one might care for; to fear for the day when the '64 station wagon (130,000 miles) will break down — "you have to have a car out here"; and not to be able to repair the damage done to one's home by a recent earthquake, much less clean the carpet or reupholster the furniture. The change in the family fortunes is marked by the place on the living-room wall where an ongoing paint job was cut off last year, along with the Apollo contract.

Specially worrisome to Frank and Dorothy White is their inability to pay for needed therapy for their five-year-old daughter, who suffers from speech and perception problems. She has been diagnosed as "a typical aphasiac." The child psychologist who has been seeing her has kindly cut his fee a bit and is letting the bill ride — "It's up to about $500" — but the child is now able to get only one hour a week of therapy instead of the desirable two hours. Moreover, she needs special preparation if she is to fit into first grade next fall, but the $300-a-month rate for private nursery school is far beyond the family's means. So Dorothy gives part of each day to tutoring her five-year-old and feels guilty about neglecting her three-year-old. She is somewhat anxious about her daughters falling behind: "These days most children already know how to read and add when they start school."

One might assume that such difficulties would turn lukewarm Republicans like Frank and Dorothy away from the party in power. But there is another dimension to their situation. They feel most uncomfortable on welfare: "The whole damned system is not designed for us. It doesn't pay enough to maintain the standard of living we had before ... You hate to go on it. They delve into your personal affairs, tell you what to do.... It destroys individual initiative. I feel guilty about taking it...."

Frank speaks of himself and his fellow engineers as "highly skilled, highly trained men" — not, emphatically, your run-of-the-mill welfare specimen. Dorothy is very much aware of the contrast between her family and the families she thinks of as welfare cases: "We're just a little bit too well off. We have just a little bit too much.... On the long lines at the medical center, they look at you like you just don't belong there. We're too well dressed, I guess."

The Whites' caseworker has routinely ordained that the family requires $390 a month to get along; their welfare benefits have been pegged at $239 a month, so Frank is permitted to earn the remaining $151 and continue to draw his welfare allotment. For every additional dollar that he earns, however, he loses a dollar of aid. At present, he has a part-time job, taking inventory in supermarkets. It pays $2.50 an hour. Thus, whether he counts cans for 15 hours a week or for 35 hours, he still ends up with a total of $390 at the end of the month. "There's no incentive to go out," he complains.

"They're telling you, you can't earn," says Dorothy, and adds, not without a touch of pride, "Frank isn't the sort of person to sit idle. We don't have that attitude of collecting without working. We've met our obligations." Frank takes as many hours of work as he can get and does odd jobs for neighbors in his spare time, but the Whites know that not every welfare client exerts himself for no profit. Indeed, Frank is convinced that the welfare rolls are filled with cheaters, and he suspects that he is now suffering because the state coffers have been plundered by others, people less diligent and fastidious than himself.

Dorothy has learned some of the difficulties of bringing up three young children on a welfare budget — "a school outfit for the oldest, one pair of pajamas each, one play outfit each, one pair of tennis shoes; they wear them out so quickly" — but she has read of women who exist on Aid to Dependent Children payments . . . and yet continue to have babies. She doesn't understand that mode of life. "The state just ought to tell them, 'No, you're not going to get a penny. So stop it!' Paddle their fannies; they're irresponsible." She believes there ought to be a cut-off point: After the birth of more than one illegitimate child, the mother would be sterilized.

So misfortune in the White household has not bred solidarity with the underprivileged, or compassion for the underclass. For all the best efforts of a local left-wing group which put Frank on its mailing list and invited him to speak on the subject of unemployment under capitalism, no radical sentiments have been aroused. Instead Frank and Dorothy are beginning to feel a kind of bitterness. Having worked hard and paid their way all their lives without asking for a great deal as things go in America, they resent being lumped with people who have made careers of living off welfare. It is easier to call up sympathy for the poor when one's own circumstances do not tax one's resources of sympathy; there is only so much of that good thing to go around.

The Whites know their blessings — a cozy home in a quiet, all white suburb, a decent school, hopes for a new job despite the gloomy smog that has closed in on the aerospace business. (Although he seems to have mastered the knack of not looking too far into the future, Frank does toy with a last-resort notion of moving to Tasmania if the smog doesn't lift.) They see their situation as a temporary one, an accident which must in the nature of things be corrected. "We're not being destroyed by this," affirms Dorothy. And she goes on to compare their own lifelong willingness to work — Frank was an orphan who got his BS at the University of Texas on the GI Bill — and their determination to keep their family together no matter what, with those she calls irresponsible, the people who seem content to live indefinitely on handouts and whose loudest complaint is that the handouts aren't big enough. Nothing she has seen at the medical center has forced her to change her image of welfare clients.

Perhaps the feelings of Frank and Dorothy White are not typical. They do, after all, live in a congressional district that has sent Barry Goldwater's son to Washington. Perhaps elsewhere affection for the poor abounds in the world of the formerly well-off, and perhaps other workers displaced from the aerospace industry are more worried about the military-industrial complex and the environmental perils of the SST than they are about their own jobs. Perhaps. But this century's history does not lack examples of a hurt, confused, angry middle class moving not to the Left along with a hurt, confused, angry lower class, but to the distant Right. Dorothy, though not very political (she couldn't recall the name of her congressman), admits to an admiration for Governor Ronald Reagan.

Adversity generally breeds discontent — but it does not channel it. That is accomplished by other influences, the kind of influences that are making themselves felt on the Whites. Frank and Dorothy are not blaming the System for their troubles. They don't know exactly who or what to blame, outside of bad luck, but they want it clearly understood that they do not belong on welfare. In their small way, they represent an American success story. They are part of the System, not dropouts or flunkouts, and if it comes to a division, they will not, if they can help it, be found in the ranks of the dispossessed.

We are imposing impossible options. In our society, the ability to feed, clothe, and shelter one's children, one's wife, and oneself depends in most cases on one's ability to find and hold a job. If jobs are not available for all who want them, people will cheat, connive, and lie in order to keep a job. It is easy to adopt a high moral tone if one's income is secure. It is not so easy when the *alternative* is to fail to provide for one's wife and children.

This book examines an option which could be developed. It would maintain income — provide Committed Spending — to those who have held good jobs paying decent incomes over a period of time. The proposed pattern would provide people with the freedom to change careers, to pursue their education, to carry on activities which they themselves feel are important. This scheme would be devised to work in parallel with a guaranteed income or to use an alternative term which I prefer — Basic Economic Security. (For further discussion of Basic Economic Security, see my books, *Free Men and Free Markets* and *The Guaranteed Income*. For an over-all discussion of the economic/ecological issues of today, see my *Economizing Abundance*.)

We need to develop new choices. The present system forces people to act narrowly within existing norms — they fear to take imaginative and creative steps because they might lose their jobs. If we enact Basic Economic Security and Committed Spending and thus provide people with assured resources, many people will be freed to act creatively. The knowledge that there are alternative options will enable some people to take time to imagine the future and others to act in the present so as to create new institutions which will aim at melding the past with the future. Those who do remain within the present private and governmental structures will increasingly do so because they perceive the real value of their actions; they will see that they are conserving and promoting the energy-producing dynamic of the industrial-era socioeconomy so that it can be used to create the communications era.

The underlying assumption in this book is that our society is in transition: a "passage from one state, stage, place, or subject to another." (Webster) When the essays in this book were first written, five or six years ago, the process of transition was more gradual than it is now and the role of the middle class in the transition was therefore presented primarily in socioeconomic and personal terms. It was then considered vitally necessary to prevent economic breakdown during the period of transition by providing income maintenance to this group. It was hoped that this would prevent a sociocultural gulf developing between "those in the productive system and those outside it" (1968 Preface) and "provide greater freedom to those with ideas about the creation of a desirable future." (Afterword) The essays recognize the reality that in a time of rapid transitions many of those in the middle-class have a major contribution to make: they are the conservers of the ongoing socioeconomic dynamic which is one of the sources of the energy for the transition.

As the speed-up in the process of transition has increased, we need to think in new terms. We must recognize the reality of the widening gap between where we are and where we should be. In order to bridge this gap, some must decide *where* to build, some must be *engaged* in the process of bridge building, and some must *supply* energy and materials.

We are engaged in a task never previously attempted — a conscious transition from one era to another. Previous transitions from hunting and gathering to agriculture and from agriculture to industry have been essentially unconscious and major disasters were largely avoided because considerable periods of time were available and the cultures of the world were not closely interconnected. We are now moving from the industrial era to the communications era and we must make this shift in much less than one generation. Basic Economic Security and Committed Spending are minimal requirements for a successful transition.

* * *

There are many who argue that there is nothing new in the unemployment situation — that unemployment has always been part of any economic system and that no change need be anticipated within the foreseeable future. In reality, however, it is now clear that this point of view is invalid. The possibility of jobs for all is completely dependent on the continuation of the growth ethic. This ethic is now under increasing attack because of our growing understanding of the nature of ecological systems. I am personally convinced that the goal of full employment is obsolete and impossible of achievement and that the reality of unemployment — and consequent dispossession — will strike more and more people in coming years.

If the rich countries and the world are to survive, we are going to have to come to understand in the very near future that ecological concerns and a continued drive for economic growth cannot be meshed. We have not yet made significant progress in changing our fundamental perceptions.

The most obvious demonstration of the continuance of our existing attitudes came with the wage-price freeze in 1971. President Nixon was confronted with a situation of excessive inflation *and* excessive unemployment. To deal with it, he needed to increase the demand for goods and services and to decrease the pressure for wage and price increases. There were many routes which the government could theoretically have taken to achieve these purposes. The choice it made was to cut still further the taxes paid by those rich enough to buy cars — reducing taxes most for those buying the most expensive cars. At the same time, President Nixon delayed his welfare reforms, which he had previously announced as one of his urgent goals.

It is difficult to conceive of a clearer demonstration of our continuing commitment to old priorities. It is already clear that we must develop substitutes for the private car — not only because of the environmental damage it causes, but also because a system of transportation completely dependent on the private automobile deprives both young and old of adequate mobility. In addition, the decision to increase the effective purchasing power of those who are richer at the cost of the urgent needs of the poor still further skewed the pattern of income distribution.

I should make it clear at this point that I am *not* arguing that the President and the government could afford politically to act in a way significantly different from their chosen pattern of action. Indeed, my point is *precisely* the opposite. All of us, those who govern and those who are governed, are constrained by a set of mythologies and a set of socioeconomic beliefs derived from the industrial era. These determine our thinking — and therefore our actions. Only the recognition that our present mythologies and beliefs are no longer relevant or useful will permit us to change significantly the future course of America and the other rich countries.

We can only learn to balance economic necessities with an ecological perspective by achieving a new understanding of the operation of internal and international socioeconomic and ecological systems. If we are to prevent a complete split between the rich and the poor — both internally and globally — we must recognize the true forces which are presently determining "who gets what."

Economists still act as though people earn what they are worth. Rather, economic decisions should be based on the recognition that the distribution of income in the world results from the amount of power that individuals, groups, institutions, and countries have to demand resources. For example, the ability of the building trades to increase their wages far faster than other groups would appear to the non-economist to be closely related to the structure of the building industry and the power the building unions possess. The man-in-the-street is not clear about how this obvious point can be ignored by economists when they argue that incomes reflect, more or less, economic contribution. Sometimes the real world is comprehensible only to those who know no economic theory.

Economic theories about the distribution of income are derived from neo-classical theory developed in the 1870s.

The "neo-classicists" studied what would happen under certain "idealized" conditions. Economists showed that if, *and only if*, certain assumptions were met it could then be proved that each person would receive the amount of money he was "worth." These assumptions are:
— All firms are small.
— There are no labor unions.
— There is no government intervention in the economy.
— Anybody can obtain the information he requires to make intelligent decisions.

In effect, the first three of these assumptions effectively define a society without power. Neo-classicists therefore succeeded in proving the obvious — they showed that if we define away the possibility of using power, then power *cannot by definition* be used to influence the distribution of income. Of course, if power cannot be used it is reasonable to state that the distribution of income is essentially "just."

There is no need to stress the unreasonableness of such a set of assumptions as a reflection of real conditions in the early 1970s. Power exists and it is used. Rich individuals are usually more powerful than poor. Those who are working are usually more powerful than those who are too old or too young or too ill-educated to hold jobs. The rich countries are usually more powerful than the poor. Unionized workers are usually more powerful than the non-unionized and some unions are more powerful than others.

We shall never deal with the reality of the growing split between the possessed and the dispossessed until we recognize that power is the single most important determinant of the distribution of rights to resources. Fortunately, for the process of understanding, this point is being dramatized through the action of the wage and price control boards. Exceptions are granted to those who have the power to disrupt the system if their demands are not granted. The unimportant and powerless receive the amount proscribed by the law or even less. We shall find it more difficult in the future to ignore the reality of power in determining the realities of resource distribution.

The coal strike in Britain in January-February 1972 dramatized what must be expected throughout the industrialized world if we refuse to understand the seriousness and depth of this issue. One of the most necessary cements required to hold a culture together is a feeling that the distribution of effort and reward is fair. The coal strike in Britain demonstrated that there is no longer any such agreement. It demonstrated further that the degree of frustration in Britain is so great that there is a willingness to bring the country to a halt rather than stop the strike. Even more significantly, when the shortages of coal and power became acute, the population pressured the government to settle for higher wage and salary increases rather than reacting against the disruption caused by the miners.

It is critical that we understand in the near future that we have no theory and no practical methods for distributing income justly. We need to create new ones if we are to ensure the survival of the world.

* * *

A very brief concluding note. I am aware that economists will argue that this characterization has been unfair and mis-states their actual position. They will certainly claim that no economist today would argue the validity of neo-classical theory. Their rebuttal, however, would miss the point that I have been trying to make here. It is true that no economist would defend neo-classical theory. Economists *act*, however, on the basis of neo-classical theory, i.e., as if it is true. Events stem from people's actions and not from the theories that they say they hold.

ROBERT THEOBALD

PREFACE

"Who gets what?" The socially accepted answers to this crudely stated question determine much of the economic and social structure in which we live. The norms each culture develops to define rights to resources and the mechanisms that are used to enforce these rights and to permit changes in them heavily affect our patterns of conduct and our beliefs about relevant behavior.

This volume is concerned with two possible innovations in the present systems used to distribute resources in the rich countries of the world. The first is that everybody should be provided with Basic Economic Security through the availability of a guaranteed income. The second is that income-maintenance plans—Committed Spending—should be developed which would ensure that an individual who has earned an adequate income over an extended period of time would continue to receive a portion of this income. (For a brief description of these two concepts as they were set out in my book *Free Men and Free Markets,* see p. 196.)

Both of these proposals can be seen in two lights. From one angle, they appear to be desirable evolutionary steps that will enable us to deal with critical aspects of developing problems and crises: much of my previous work and some of the essays in this volume examine them in this way. From another angle, however, they appear to be basic steps to ensure the creation of the new socioeconomic order that has become essential because of man's ever-growing power to control his environment, a view developed by other essayists.

Despite the delaying tactics of those who will not study, or accept, published facts, it is abundantly clear that present systems of income distribution are breaking down. A survey published in April of 1967 showed that only 1 per cent of those on welfare were capable of being trained to hold jobs;

the rest could not reasonably be expected to find employment. Another survey published at approximately the same time showed that the percentage of people without jobs or having severe difficulty in finding jobs in inner-city ghettoes amounted to some 30 to 45 per cent and concluded that no conceivable rate of economic growth would make it possible to reabsorb these people into the economic system.

These figures confirm the views of those who have been disturbed about the impact of automation and cybernation for many years. For while economic theory makes it clear that the government can always stimulate the economy by distributing purchasing power to those who are willing to use it and thus absorb those considered as worth employing, this does not mean that everybody will continue to be "employable." An increasing number of people have been arguing that the rapid development of computer-directed machine-systems will inevitably lead to the creation of a class of "unemployables" who will not be attractive to employers at the going wage rate because a machine-system would be more efficient.

For example, the basic view of the Presidential Commission on Technology, Automation, and Economic Growth was that the labor force could be best envisaged as a line arranged in order of attractiveness of employers: the workers who were most attractive to the employer would be hired first and hiring would continue so long as there was a demand for labor. It was inevitable in the view of the commission that there would be some people who would fail to be hired because their education, skills, and talents would be inappropriate or too limited to appeal to any employer.

Unfortunately, however, this problem of unemployability is largely disguised by our present reporting systems. Levels of unemployment are reported on the basis of those who are looking for a job. The unemployable person, however, rapidly learns that there is no point in looking for a job because he cannot expect to find one: as a result he does not appear in the unemployment statistics. Our present system for reporting unemployment—particularly after its revision in January 1967—is one of the major factors that effectively prevents us from perceiving the extent of present unemployability. This can be clearly seen if we examine the situation in the depressed regions such as Appalachia where an extremely high proportion of the people have no jobs and desire jobs but where, because of the present conventions, the official statistics show a relatively low unemployment rate.

The real debate today, therefore, is no longer in terms of the possibility of unemployability; rather we are arguing about the size and scope of the problem over the short and long run. Most economists continue to believe that there is no major problem in this area. On the other hand. those concerned with cybernation—the combination of machines with computers—and cybernetics—the science of communication and control—predict that men cannot remain competitive with machines and that if they try to compete they will be reduced to slavery because they will be competing with "slave" machines. Which group of thinkers are we to believe?

Despite the fact that my own discipline is that of economics, I believe that there can be no doubt about the proper answer to this question. Conventional economists base their theories about the future course of the economy on assumptions developed by John Maynard Keynes, the great British economist, but these are fundamentally inappropriate for present conditions. Writing in the thirties Keynes ignored the factors that are now most critically important: "We take as given the existing skill and quantity of available labor, the existing quantity and quality of available equipment, the existing technique. This does not mean that we assume these facts to be constant, but merely that in this place and context, we are not considering or taking into account the effect and consequences of changes in them."

In effect, therefore, the economist is ignoring the very factors that those concerned with cybernation and cybernetics believe will be responsible for a growing problem of unemployability in the future. Economists are, in effect, assuming away those factors that would threaten the validity of their conclusions. I have yet to see any argument by an economist that effectively contradicts the position of those who are concerned with the declining competence of men, as compared to machines, in carrying out tasks where the decision-making rules can be set out in advance. Indeed, I would go further and argue that a *correct* use of economic theory actually confirms the position of the cyberneticist and the expert in cybernation. Economics has always claimed that if the cost of one factor of production increases and the cost of the other declines, there will be a movement toward greater use of the cheaper factor of production. Today, labor is getting more expensive and capital is rapidly getting less expensive: if economic theory is correct, capital will *necessarily* take the place of labor.

Acceptance of this situation leaves us with only two main choices if each individual is to be able to obtain enough money to have a decent standard of living. On the one hand, we can provide direct income rights to all who need them along the lines explored in this book. On the other hand, we can find new ways to get people into jobs and keep them there, through job training and retraining and through making the government the employer of last resort. This latter policy would require the government to make jobs available to all those who cannot find them through the normal market-mechanism.

This suggestion, which aims to keep people in some form of employment, is clearly based on the experience of the thirties when attempts were made to provide those who were unemployed with the opportunity to work in government activities until the economy should itself provide enough jobs once more. But it should be abundantly clear that the situations are *not* parallel. It was correctly anticipated in the thirties that everybody would be needed in conventional jobs again. Today, however, we are concerned with people who will never be able to hold conventional jobs, and we must deal with a situation where an ever-rising proportion of the population would have to be employed by the government in order to preserve the myth of full employment.

It is surely not difficult to imagine the end result of making government the employer of last resort. More and more of the population would be relegated to areas of activity outside the mainstream of the economy. More and more people would be condemned to dead-end activities that society could not be bothered to develop machine-systems to handle. An enormous social gulf would develop between those in the productive system and those outside it. The threat of such a development has been visible for so long that many dystopias have been written about it—today's imminent danger is that we may indeed live them.

The available alternative to such a threat is the design for economic security explored in this book. It is interesting to note that this design has also been attacked on the grounds that it would inevitably lead to a division between the various classes in the society. This, however, fails to understand the longer-run impact of the design for it would not only eliminate the necessity for money in the economy within a relatively short period but would also, as a consequence, lead to a profoundly different type of society in which class lines would be abolished. Some of the essays in this book and in *The Guaranteed Income* are relevant in this context and my own Afterword to this volume attempts to draw the threads together in such a way that they become compelling.

The fundamental issue that lies behind all of the debates in this area is whether cybernation is fundamentally changing the nature of the world in which we live. Irving Kaplan replies in the first essay with a resounding affirmative stating, to use his own words: "Whatever direction progress takes from this point on will be a dramatic one." Kaplan argues essentially that the computer is becoming so much more economical than man in a wide variety of roles that the replacement of men with limited skills and education will inevitably proceed at a very rapid rate from this point into the future.

R. Christian Anderson enlarges on this insight in his essay and shows that the impact of the new technologies on the highly educated man and woman will be traumatic unless there are profound institutional changes. He proposes methods by which Committed Spending could be employed to facilitate the movement of people between jobs and activities and shows that the availability of income as a right might well reintroduce the possibility of creativity for many presently unable to act outside their own job situation.

George Nelson further develops this insight suggesting that many of the professions presently considered to be artistic and creative actually engage in repetitive activities and that those in such professions as architecture, for example, can expect to be largely replaced by computers in the relatively near future. He also suggests some changes in patterns and styles of life that might follow from the growing availability of income rights without jobs.

The next essay, by Kendall Cochran, proves that the development of Basic Economic Security and Committed Spending requires fundamental changes in tax systems. Starting from the increasingly accepted view that the distribution of income in any country is, and must be, determined by value systems rather than by economics, he proves that many aspects of the present tax system would need fundamental reform in these new circumstances. In effect, almost all net income, less a standard exemption, would be taxed under the scheme he proposes.

The remaining essays consider some of the overall societal implications of Basic Economic Security and Committed Spending. Margaret Mead shows how the introduction of new forms of income rights would inevitably affect all social structures, ranging from the family to our views of work, from our views of the rights of various social classes to our views of the rights of those at various ages. As an anthropologist she recognizes the inevitability of total changes in the societal system and thus develops in her essay both the possibilities and problems inherent in the concept, thus clarifying the fact that new forms of income distribution are no panacea for all the problems that presently face us.

Indeed this recognition of the need for overall change is common to all the essays. New rights to income are presented throughout as a necessary precondition to living in the new world we have ourselves created, but they are not perceived as precursors of Utopia. This form of presentation will undoubtedly provide more ammunition to certain types of critics who have previously seized on any admission that new forms of income rights would not provide instant perfection. However, we must learn to examine the balance of advantage in a measure rather than looking only at its advantages if we are in favor of it or at its disadvantages if we are opposed to it.

A. A. Liveright examines in the next essay how education—particularly adult education—might be affected. He starts his analysis from the generally accepted view that adult education is presently failing to do its job and then develops the idea that we already have the capacity to begin to restructure our educational patterns along the lines suggested by modern psychological theorizing. His proposals are based on a new way of regarding the learning potentials of all human beings, whether child or adult: he argues from the assumption that we all have an inherent drive toward self-realization so long as our immediate needs are met.

Don Benson's essay stretches this argument further. He studies the implications of a world in which education has become the core reality—the method of living. He then describes the nature of the system into which we must move if we are to benefit from the technology we have ourselves created. His style and technique are different: he no longer objectively analyzes but subjectively feels what it will mean to live in this new world.

Finally, Henry Malcolm shows that the availability of abundance forces religion to realize its doctrines, to live in the present instead of the future, to take part in the realization of the gospel. He argues that Christianity has adapted so well to a world in which man was always looking *toward* the realization of the gospel that it will inevitably have enormous difficulty in living within the actuality of realized hope.

These essays seem to me to represent the coming of age of the debate on the need for fundamental changes in income distribution. There is no longer a reliance on short-run problems to force the adoption of new measures, but rather an analytical framework is being developed showing that the future shape of the society requires the breaking of the link between job and income. There is no suggestion that work will be abolished, no belief that man will be perfected, only a simple recognition that we must now design a social system in which each individual can realize his potential and his uniqueness. In effect, the authors in this volume demand a profound reversal. Today systems control people; the authors in this volume propose that institutional arrangements be designed that will effectively serve the needs of people.

ROBERT THEOBALD

July 1967.

THE IMMINENT REVOLUTION IN CYBERNATION[1]

Irving E. Kaplan

Somewhere in the order of two million years ago, one line of higher primate had adapted to upright walking, ceased to use his arms for locomotion, and developed an enlarged brain. About the same time this anthropoid began also to shape available materials into tools and to communicate in the complex symbology of speech. Work was not a new invention as many other forms of life had built nests, burrowed, or stored food, but this new anthropoid was to expand this idea significantly. As he began to work in earnest he became increasingly aware of the value of work but also increasingly tired of it. With tools and communication to produce more work for his effort, man and his technology began life together.

The first 1,995,000 years of this technical development were relatively uneventful and slow. Before long, man had developed an array of tools for striking, cutting, chopping, and prying, and had begun to use animal power. However, it wasn't until six thousand years ago that the simple lathe was developed by the Etruscans. Between five and six thousand years ago written language, bronze, and the wheel and axle were developed in the Near East. Written communication contributed to an upsurge of technology, including chemistry, mechanical devices, and structures. The first steam turbine was constructed in about 120 B.C. by Hero of Alexandria. By the sixteenth century A.D., Leonardo Da Vinci had contributed

[1] Cf. Irving E. Kaplan, "The Projected Effect of Automation on Future Navy Personnel Requirements, Part II: Implications for the Navy's Environment, The Nation," San Diego, Calif.: U. S. Naval Personnel Research Activity, August 1966.

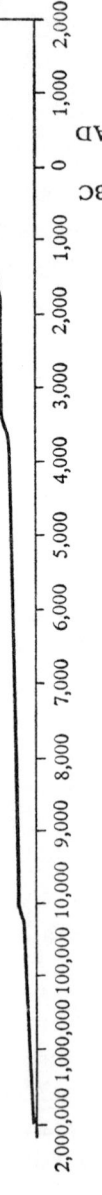

Figure 1. MAN'S CUMULATIVE TECHNICAL PROGRESS

The time scale between 10,000 and 2,000,000 years B.C. would extend the abscissa to about 400 inches if it were not compressed. The curve ends at the beginning of the nineteenth century as the rate of technical progress in the last 65 years is too great to be adequately displayed in this figure.

heavily with a number of technical designs, including a calculating machine. In 1698 Thomas Savery was drawing well water with a steam engine. By the middle of the nineteenth century another mechanical computer and railroading had become facts, and by the middle of the twentieth century the world had entered the age of atomic power, electronics, and computers.

The above is, of course, a very condensed history and its informational content is not intended to be as interesting as the trend it tries to convey. Figure 1 shows this trend graphically as a smoothed curve. The ordinate of this graph represents cumulative technical progress in numbers of important inventions and technological discoveries. The rate of invention has been so great during the first two-thirds of the twentieth century that the significance of this progress can hardly be judged relative to the earlier progress. The curve therefore ends with the beginning of our century. The importance of Figure 1 is in the exponentially accelerating rate of the technical progress depicted. This acceleration implies three interesting alternatives for the future, each of these alternatives being of a very radical nature.

The first alternative, implied if the exponential trend shown remains stable, is that the rate of progress in the technological world of the near future is beyond the comprehension of minds utilizing the contemporary frame of reference. Under this alternative we would not be far from the truth if we predicted that the next twenty years will see far more technological progress than has the previous two million years.

The average man's imagination uses only the data of experience in its operation and his mind cannot conceptualize exponential rates of progress very easily. The average man is therefore likely to approach the implications of continuous exponential progress with considerable skepticism. The second alternative may be just as difficult to accept and would be shown as a flattening of the curve to illustrate a deceleration of technical progress. A decline could be due either to the exhaustion of technological potential or to the attainment of such a high level of technology that the culture would be saturated with the technological product and society would shift its values. For any reason, a technological decline is very hard to imagine in our present state of ascending technology.

The third alternative would be for the curve to end or to fall precipitously. This could indicate only a catastrophic event such as a disease epidemic of tremendous proportions, a destructive astronomical event, or a war of sufficient destructive force to destroy the nation's or the world's industry and technology. Vivid demonstrations of atomic weaponry and twenty years of intense public consideration of this topic may have made the third alternative the least offensive to the contemporary sense of credibility. Yet the powerful implications of this alternative make it as provocative as the first two.

Our exponential curve allows for only the three alternatives we have just discussed, each being so far removed from contemporary experience as to present the individual with a problem of credibility. Whatever direction progress takes from this point on will be a dramatic one. The remainder of this essay contains a presentation of information and inference that fully supports this prediction of imminent and dramatic changes to the nation.

THE REVOLUTION IN ELECTRONICS

Regardless of the apparent purpose, most technology relieves man of physical and mental work. Thus technology is, in a very large sense, automation. This essay, however, will be centrally concerned with that aspect of automation using computers to control the machines of industry, government, education, and research, and to perform data-processing operations previously considered "mental work." This type of automation has been aptly labeled "cybernation."[2] Modern computers are based on electronic technology, and an understanding of the impending status of computers will require an understanding of the revolutionary state of affairs in the electronics industry.

Although semiconductor devices existed prior to 1900, it was not until 1948 that the transistor was invented and not until 1959–1961 that such solid state electronic devices were developed to the point where they could replace short-lived and fragile tubes and be militarily and industrially useful.

The advent of solid state devices is significant, not only as the beginning of a revolution in electronics, but also as an illustration of the substantial amount of time required between the invention of the basic device and its development to the point of commercial usefulness. Between 1959 and the present, the electronics industry, substantially aided by military research and support, has been working toward the perfection of circuits that would provide the following desirable attributes:

1. A reduction of volume and weight.
2. Fewer discrete components and connections.
3. Reduced power requirements.
4. Reduced requirements for cooling.
5. Increased producibility and reduced costs.
6. Increased reliability.
7. Increased maintainability.

In general, three approaches were followed toward these achievements. The oldest approach is the miniaturization of discrete components, construction, and packaging. The second approach, thin films, is the deposition of thin metallic and dielectric films on small dielectric wafers to form circuits

[2] The term cybernation was devised from Norbert Wiener"s neologism "cybernetics" and from "automation" (also a relatively new word) by Donald Michael in his pamphlet *Cybernation: The Silent Conquest*, Santa Barbara, Calif.: Center for the Study of Democratic Institutions, 1962.

that integrate all but the active functions (i.e. transistors and diodes), which must presently be manually attached. The third approach, integrated semiconductor circuitry, utilizes small chips of semiconductor material, silicon or metal oxides, which are processed via vacuum infusion of various impurities (dopes) through masks to form complete circuits within the chip.

Of the three approaches to miniaturization, the semiconductor approach has been the most successful for the greatest variety of purposes. Microelectronic semiconductor (integrated) circuits are mass produced via automation at costs that range in the small fractions of a cent per component equivalent.[3] Each circuit, perhaps .1 inch wide, .25 inch long (many as small as .030 inch on a side), and a few thousandths of an inch thick, then has the lead wires welded on and is packaged.

Total production costs for these early circuits have been reported to run at less than a dollar, even for the most complex circuits. Such early military and industrial integrated circuits were being sold in 1964 for prices that had been reduced by magnitudes of a hundred to a thousand times as compared with the equivalent conventional circuits sold in 1960. At present, however, integrated circuits still cannot be produced at such low costs to provide electrical values of the close tolerances needed for precision linear systems like radars and analogue computers. This has led integrated circuits to be identified with digital applications, which require less precision. By early 1964, a military linear system, the LORAN AN/ARN-78 Navigation Receiver was redesigned into a digital receiver and a successful prototype constructed of nonprecision integrated circuits. Since this pioneer achievement,

[3] Because the electronic functions of integrated semiconductor circuits are produced by integral three-dimensional patterns rather than by discrete components such as resistors, capacitors, and transistors we must refer to component "equivalents" if we are to compare microelectronics with conventional circuitry.

the military has committed a number of systems, which would formerly have been linear, to digital design. It therefore seems highly probable that the segment of the electronics industry that produces military and industrial equipment will swing over to digital design in a major way. Although microelectronic circuits are not capable of handling the high power required for such applications as radio and radar transmission, the industry has recently achieved small, cheap, and highly reliable transistor devices, which can replace the expensive and unreliable high-power tubes presently in use. The day is close when even high-power high-frequency equipment will be compact, strong, highly reliable, and inexpensive. The sale of cheap, long-lasting electronic appliances on the consumer market is not close at hand, however, as this could destroy the economic principle of obsolescence under which the industry operates.

Microelectronic systems possess each of the attributes listed earlier to a degree that was unanticipated during the early stages of research and development. Despite the attributes implied by the name of the new technology, the most important aspects of microelectronics are not the reduction of size and weight so much as the tremendous reduction in production costs and the tremendous increase in the life of the equipment (present estimates being that integrated circuits can last 100,000 years).[4] Although the production costs of circuits such as amplifiers, oscillators, logic circuits, etc., have been reduced by factors in the magnitude of a thousand, it is anticipated that refined production techniques, high production runs, and the greater integration of circuits into large monolithic units (possibly single monolithic equipments or systems) will reduce production costs even more.

The trend toward the production of both components (integrated circuits) and systems by the same producer is more than the mere expression of economic feasibility. The next

[4] W. R. Boehm, "Microelectronics," *Bureau of Ships Journal,* November 1964.

logical step beyond the production of a single circuit function in a chip is to produce two or more functions per chip. Besides lowering the cost of circuit production and packaging by "fantastic" margins, greater integration results in an even smaller product, and, most important, reduces the number of connections thereby increasing the life of the system. High levels of integration are therefore sought after by the Defense Department, the rationale being that the cost of highly integrated systems will be sufficiently small, the reliability sufficiently high, and the reduction in maintenance requirements (shops, logistics, equipment, personnel, training, etc.) so great that whole equipments or sections of equipment may be thrown away and replaced at significant savings and greater operational effectiveness when (and if) they fail. Possible problems presented by this "large circuit" concept are that electronic equipment will require much custom design as compared with systems constructed from standardized "off the shelf" circuit components. Complex monolithic integrations will present new problems in design and fabrication. However, since monolithic integration is especially feasible for digital computer circuitry, greater and greater reductions will be made in the costs of computer production as progress is made toward optimal integration. Of great significance for the military and for industry is the fact that low cost and small size will result in systems that are capable of remaining in operation despite failures in any parts of the system. For instance, the reduced size and weight of electronic systems will enable an airplane, a ship, or even an industrial plant to have redundant (duplicate) systems distributed throughout its structure. Thus, dispersed redundancy can provide protection from loss of system function due both to electronic failure and events such as fire, collision, and even earthquake.

Whatever the level of integration, e.g. single function circuits or completely monolithic equipments, the skills and knowledges now associated with electronic repair and maintenance will no longer be required. Complex systems using even small functional circuits can be tested and repaired simultaneously by unskilled personnel who can systematically replace plug-in modules until the system is again functioning, the bad modules being thrown away. It is theoretically possible, and becoming more and more feasible, to design many electromechanical devices such as synchro- and servo-mechanisms out of systems via techniques such as digital design, and to replace many electromechanical functions with electronic functions. Those electromechanical devices that will be required are already incorporating lubricants, plastics, insulation materials, design and production methods which make it possible to build devices that are much smaller, require much less servicing, and are much more reliable than devices of just a few years ago.

In summary, then, the direct consequences of the microelectronic revolution will be to automate electronic repair and maintenance as we now know it out of existence.

THE REVOLUTION IN COMPUTERS

As significant as are the direct consequences of microelectronics on work, the indirect consequences are even greater. As we have indicated, semiconductor circuitry is especially suitable for application to digital equipment. Because digital computers utilize a great redundancy of circuits the benefits of cheap mass producibility of integrated circuits are greatly increased, and automated circuit production is of very special economic importance in the manufacture of computers. Thus, microelectronic computers, less expensive, smaller, faster, more tolerant of environmental variations, consuming less power, dissipating less heat, and more reliable by many magnitudes, will also be much cheaper to produce; and the computer producer who does not use microelectronic construction to its maximum will be at a severe disadvantage. As expected, some microelectronic computers are already on the market and more are being developed. This is the beginning of a new breed of inexpensive and reliable control and data-processing mechanisms that will tremendously reduce the feasibility of retaining human workers in the administrative, productive, and distributive processes of all industry, agriculture, and government; domestic and foreign.

THE IMMEDIATE LOGIC FOR CYBERNATION

Microelectronic computers produced for government and industrial consumption in the immediate future will usually be constructed from small semiconductor circuits containing one or a few functions. Mass production of these circuits has already resulted in circuit costs that are about .1 per cent of the costs of conventional printed circuits using discrete solid state components. Chassis construction and packaging of these early computers do not depart radically from the conventional industrial and military "rack and plug-in" techniques, so that assembly costs per volume of equipment will not change significantly. Thus, if the circuitry of a conventional computer used for specialized industrial cybernation costs 80 to 90 per cent of the total system (minus memory care and peripheral equipment), the total production cost of a comparative microelectronic system should be in the order of .7 to 1.3 per cent of the cost of a conventional system (allowing for the reduction in the amount of chassis, cabinetry, cooling equipment, and associated hardware required by the microelectronic circuitry). These computers will not require wages, will perform much faster, for longer sustained periods of time, and will require less time to find and repair failures. They will not have troublesome emotions, will not require supervision, and will not require long periods of time to be trained and brought up to optimal proficiency. Thus, the lowered cost per unit work, the increase in reliability, and the increase in productivity by cybernated manufacturing and "white collar" systems will make cybernation an absolutely essential factor in economic competition.

The application of computers to industrial processes, however, does require additional equipment. In many cases a manually operated production machine can be converted to computer control by the addition of control mechanisms that translate control signals from the computer into machine functions. More frequently it is most feasible to redesign complete production systems, changing the machines, tools, process, and even product so as to take greatest advantage of automation techniques. For instance, the production of mechanical components conventionally requires the design of the component, a set of drawings, determinations as to which machines to use in what order, and a succession of machining processes. Modern production factories have combined many machining processes into a single machine complex that can be mechanically programmed to produce the finished item from a casting or from raw stock. The state-of-the-art now exists that will enable the designer to write a program of sequential processes by which a unitary computer-controlled multipurpose machine complex will produce a given number of machined and assembled items without human labor. Feedback will enable the machine to maintain tolerance despite tool wear and to switch new tools into place when required. Time sharing of processes may even enable such a multipurpose machine complex to produce a number of different items at the same time, thus making better use of the number and variety of tools and processes built into the complex.

The design and construction of such systems would be expensive if produced as special-purpose production complexes. Produced as multipurpose machines, however, they can theoretically be used to reproduce themselves for a large multipurpose market. The more versatile the machines are, the greater the market. Thus the demand for such machine complexes would be enlarged due to the decreased cost of volume production; the versatility to the user, making it an investment with a surer payoff potential; the reduction in volume of machinery and space required to produce a unit item; the tremendous reduction in labor and supervisory costs; the reduction in administrative requirements; and the decrease in production time required per unit item.

Thus it appears that despite the addition of computers and control equipment, the reduction in the amount of production machinery required to produce the product may even lower the initial cost of fully automated production systems, especially after the design and development costs for such systems are amortized. The ensuing reductions in production costs brought about by such systems are, however, the main factor in the expansion of industrial automation.

In early 1964 the largest producer of computers, IBM, marketed the 360, a computer system that is 100 per cent microelectronic. This system has already been modified from a thin film technology (the more expensive method) to integrated semiconductor circuitry (although it has been reported that many of the thin film circuits cost as little as 12 cents to produce). By July of 1965, Univac, another producer of computers, had contracted to Fairchild Semiconductor for integrated semiconductor circuits that were estimated by the *Wall Street Journal* to be equal to 70 per cent of the industry's total microelectronic production to that time. As of the last revision of this article (April 1967) reports and advertisements in the industrial journals indicate that at least five producers are marketing microelectronic computers for industrial control and data processing.

The electronics industry is in a very rapid state of flux. New corporations and divisions have been born out of the microelectronic revolution and every major producer of electronics has started to use the new technology. A number of component producers have started to produce sections, subsystems, and complete systems; and some who designed and built prototype systems to demonstrate the microelectronic technology went on to become system producers because microelectronics simplifies system construction and the capital investment required to build these systems is not great. On the other hand, the large scale producers of systems entered the production of circuits because this offered the logical area of reinvestment, because it was required to ensure the availability of integrated circuits, and because the production of systems by component producers was an economic threat that had to be met. It appears, therefore, that the trend is toward the merging of the component and system production industries, a trend favorable to the ultimate production and marketing of monolithic units of equipment such as computers. Since microelectronic circuitry is so easily producible, inexpensive, and long lived, it is evident that severe competition in the electronics industry will soon result in the elimination of many producers unless world markets expand greatly.

TO WHAT EXTENT AUTOMATION?

For our purposes, we have defined automation as the aspect of technology that reduces man's labor. Thus if construction forms for homes or commercial structures are assembled out of standardized components that can be recombined in many configurations, hydraulic and electrical conduit and equipments are installed, and foamed plastic molded in the forms, this is automated building construction. Products that wear longer, rapid-transit systems that reduce walking and driving, and standardized consumer items that require fewer technological resources are also forms of automation. It is anticipated that the extensive utilization of cybernated manufacturing, data processing, and military systems will bring about a greater cultural awareness and appreciation of system and efficiency, and these values will pervade every aspect of man's behavior. Thus cybernation will spur the advance of automation in all aspects of human life, including many functions in which computers will not be utilized.

In an effort to predict the extent to which automation will replace human labor, an analysis was made of five hundred occupations randomly chosen from the *Dictionary of Occupational Titles* (D.O.T.) published by the United States Employment Service. Each of the five hundred occupational definitions was judged in light of the researcher's knowledge of occupations and automation techniques.[5] Each occupation was judged as belonging in one or more of the following categories: (a) entirely replaceable by automation and standardization, (b) entirely prone to obsolescence because of the elimination of the need for the item or process by technical change and invention, (c) partially replaceable by automation, (d) not replaceable by automation and not likely to become absolescent to any significant extent, and (e) too unique or "small" (i.e. few practitioners) an occupation to require automation and therefore not prone to obsolescence. The five categories were then summed up into three general categories showing those occupations judged to be entirely displaceable, partially reduceable, and strongly resistant to automation. Table 1 presents the results of the analysis.

Those occupations considered displaceable by automation and new technology were mainly found as functions in sizable industrial systems such as steelmaking, shoe production, or the chemical industry. Those occupations considered reducable or partially replaceable by automation included jobs such as deputy police chief, gravity prospecting observer, and others such as are found in the butchering industry. It was felt that these occupations included skills that would resist all but the most complex and expensive automation and that the industrial functions performed would still be required in the foreseeable future.

[5] The validity of the judgments made is based on the researcher's twelve years of experience in industrial placement, civilian and military occupational research, and two years of research on automation techniques.

TABLE 1

Five Hundred Randomly Chosen Occupations: Judgments of Proneness to Automation or Obsolescence Due to Technological Change

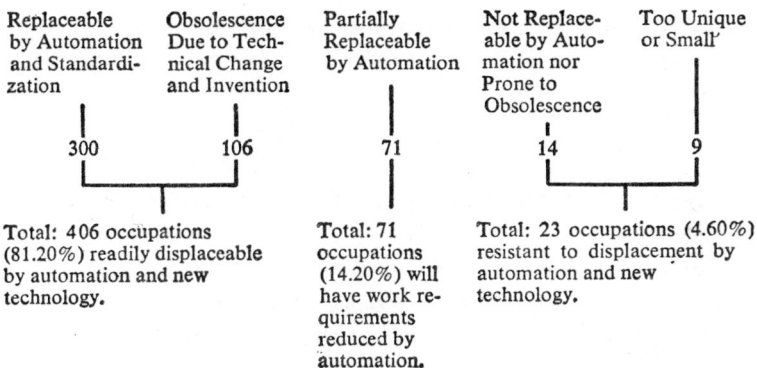

Total: 406 occupations (81.20%) readily displaceable by automation and new technology.

Total: 71 occupations (14.20%) will have work requirements reduced by automation.

Total: 23 occupations (4.60%) resistant to displacement by automation and new technology.

The occupations considered not prone to displacement or obsolescence in the moderate future were judged to produce objects with a value as art or handicraft; to require creativity; complex heuristic thought processes, and complex knowledge-skill combinations. These occupations also included those man values for himself. In this category were included such diverse occupations as astronomer and tree grafter. In addition, the last occupational category included small custom industries and services, which were judged too small to automate profitably.

The five hundred judgments of Table 1 were based on a knowledge of contemporary occupations on the one hand and a knowledge of contemporary automation methods on the other. The researcher had no claim to the technical excellence and ingenuity that would be required to determine whether or not the occupations deemed resistant to automation and obsolescence on the basis of the contemporary state-of-the-art of cybernation will not succumb to imminent invention.

In light of the trend displayed in Figure 1 and because the researcher's judgments will almost surely fall short of the technical ingenuity abundant in industry, it is felt that the judgments presented in Table 1 are conservative but that they do present an idea of the magnitude of the occupational displacement that can be expected from the new state-of-the-art in the near future. Eventually, all processes should succumb to Norbert Wiener's precept of the universal applicability of cybernetics.

PREDICTION OF INDUSTRIAL PROGRESS

Scientific and technical progress is exceedingly difficult to predict over any useful period of time because significant breakthroughs and advances occur in an unscheduled and serendipitous manner. Also, such progress is very often "keep from the market" as it may be disadvantageous to the economy or security of the controlling party. The progress and impact of cybernation, however, can be predicted with relative accuracy for the next decade because of the forces at work which will give cybernation a direction and impetus.

As we have said, an electronic state-of-the-art, indicative of the imminent production and marketing of a new breed of computers, has been achieved. If the supply and demand principle is allowed to work, the demand for cybernation will rise in response to the lowered cost of these computers, and this raises the problem of availability and adequacy of programming or softwear. Will the softwear be able to keep up with the requirements of burgeoning cybernation? It might appear that unless programmer training is expanded programmers will soon be in very short supply. However, this question is more complex than it at first appears. The expanding use of computers in all areas of application will require many new programs. Even existing programs are very often changed because of computer changes, advances in programming technology, and changes to the content areas being programmed. In general, progress seems to imply an unending requirement for new programs. On the other hand, many softwear experts believe that a majority of the programs that will be needed in the next few years already exist, the problem being to find these programs, translate them from one machine language to another as required, and adapt them for whichever special purpose may be required. These functions are now being automated. Data retrieval systems are making the programs more available (in many cases direct transmission of programs from one computer or storage facility to another over the telephone system) and compiler programs are translating and converting basic programs to the language and special application required. Many programming requirements are being met by cutting and recombining segments of the existing fund of program material.

The expansion of computer applications will therefore require some new programs. As cybernation expands, however, it can be expected that the cybernation of cybernation will expand also. Thus, except for experimental or developmental applications, the problem of programming for the surge of new computers may not be as great as anticipated.

The cheap and plentiful computer will find immediate utilization in the "white collar" data-processing area. In addition to the computer and its peripheral equipment (displays, printers, manual input devices, tape transports, memory storage equipment, etc.) little new technology will be required to cybernate most office functions.

THE EFFECTS OF THE MICROELECTRONIC COMPUTER
ON ORGANIZATIONS AND INDUSTRY

On the assumption that all systematic processes can be cybernetically controlled it appears that much of industry, commerce, education, the military and other government functions, and the practicing arts and sciences are subject to nearly complete cybernation. Notably not presently or foreseeably prone to automation are those forward fringes of each field of endeavor in which are created and expanded the body of knowledge and practice (discovery, invention, and lawmaking).[6]

The remaining question is one of economic feasibility. Will the lowered computer prices (see *Appendix* to this article) be sufficient to induce a large scale acceleration of cybernation? If the economy were static the practicality of such recapitalization might be questionable. However, the expanding economy provides the opportunity to expand via cybernation. In addition, requirements for retooling and reorganization also provide a constant opportunity to cybernate. In many instances the low cost of highly reliable cybernated systems, combined with their greater production efficiency, will make the change from even a well-running human-operated system to a cybernated system extremely profitable.

Initial installation of microelectronic cybernation will in itself spur the further acceleration of cybernation in two ways. First, it will enable cybernated production of cybernation systems, which will reduce their market prices even further. Second, the use of highly efficient cybernation by one pro-

[6] Much effort has been given toward the conceptualization of systems capable of perceiving, learning, thinking, and creating. To date, a number of conceptual models for these functions have been constructed. Systems operating on these models are able to correct inappropriate behavior via trial and error, recognize simple visual patterns, and think a good game of checkers and a very moderate game of chess. It presently appears that machine mentation, if it is to approach human capabilities, will require computers of enormous sensory, logical, and mnemonic capacities. Models for computer creativity are based on the concept that novelty can be brought about by random recombination of data already existing in the computer's memory or being acquired into the computer. In order to approach a human-like capability for creativity, the computer would have to acquire a voluminous set of criteria for goodness or truth in whatever area it is specializing in, or it must have discovered or been programmed with a (set of) "basic unifying principle(s)."

ducer will require competition via the same route by the other producers in the industry. Under such competition, those producers not sufficiently capitalized to cybernate will fail.

For many years the trend in management has been toward the establishment of an increasing reliance on management technology. The earlier movement toward "scientific management" and the latest inroads into all levels of management by operations-analysis techniques are indicative of the systematization taking place. This trend will be accelerated by microelectronic computers, which will be able to control or coordinate large, fragmented, and diverse organizations. It seems likely, therefore, that the trend in organizations of all types will be toward centralization.

Systematization as presently known has a stabilizing influence. If production efficiency is the prime requirement, the stability of a system must be maintained and change must be ignored or suppressed. In addition to the relationship between efficiency and the stability of organizational and societal systems, the individual also seeks stability in varying degrees to enhance his own operational efficiency. Many management personnel seek stability to minimize requirements on time and effort (maintain efficiency), to maintain the structures they have built as a source of personal satisfaction, and to avoid the threats and challenges that change brings.

Computers will not only make a high degree of systematization possible but will also make it possible for systems to become dynamic and capable of constant change. Computers can be constructed and programmed to detect, analyze, evaluate, (in accordance with present values and criteria) and adapt the system to change. Within limits it may even be possible for a computer to make changes to a system so as to initiate growth, maintain consumer interest, counteract weather changes, or fulfill other purposes. But whether or not machines will ever be capable of initiating change in response to complex conditions or whether they can be developed to the point of being truly creative, it is felt that important decisions will remain within the province of man's work. Not because man's ultimate judgment is better or because consent must be obtained from man's value structure and emotional needs (these can, conceptually, also be programmed into the computer), but because man must work also. Feeling responsible and important appears to be a basic need that man can best fulfill by being causative.

THE ACCELERATION OF CYBERNATION: A SCHEDULE

Figure 1 shows a trend that, if maintained, predicts a tremendous acceleration of technical progress for the twentieth century. With two-thirds of the century gone the prediction is already upheld by any measure one may wish to use. The exponential curve shown is not meant as evidence in support of the use of trend predictions, but rather as a demonstration intended to make the great acceleration of automation, which is indicated from the previous discussions, more credible.

The summer of 1964 saw the introduction of the microelectronic IBM 360 complex on the market. The reduction in production costs was very impressive.

By 1967 a number of other microelectronic computers had appeared (mainly for the military and for space use).

By the spring of 1967 a number of major producers were marketing microelectronic computers for industry. The costs of industrial computers should therefore drop very significantly if the market remains competitive.

Between 1965 and 1970 the circuits in computers will become more and more integrated, reducing both circuit unit and assembly costs. Computer production methods will become more efficient due to refinement and increased demand. Cybernation by some producers will require all producers to cybernate if they are to remain competitive. Barring illegal agreements among producers or the formation of trusts, this period will see the intense expansion of cybernation in industry and commerce, with increases also in areas such as government and education. The latter part of this period may see the Soviet Union bidding for buyers on many world markets with goods produced by cybernation. Countries such as West Germany, France, and Great Britain will also stiffen trade competition with the products of their cybernated industry. The distribution of wealth to the population, or the control of this function, will become an irreversible major function of government.

By 1972, allowing one to six years to design and build cybernated production systems, a large majority of the nation's jobs now in existence will be obsolete.

By 1980 the present economic system will have changed so radically as to be unrecognizable. The political system may not change much but political issues will have changed immensely. The culture, including institutions such as marriage, education, work, and recreation will have changed radically or will be in the process of rapid change.

The above forecast appears so radical as to tax credulity. However, it is supported by the present technology and by the theory of economic competition and is predictable from the exponential curve in Figure 1. We have simply reached the point of radical events for which history cannot provide a model. Those who have defended the concept that automation does not create unemployment [7,8,9] have done so on the basis of historical trend evidence. It has been shown that a sufficient number of new jobs are created by the new con-

[7] Charles Silberman, "The Real News About Automation," *Fortune*, January 1965.
[8] Ralph W. Ells, "Is Automation Causing Our High Unemployment?" *Personnel*, July–August 1963.
[9] Daniel Bell, "The Bogey of Automation," *The New York Review*, August 26, 1965.

sumer demands generated by affluence and by new products, by the labor required to build the machinery of automation, and by the material requirements of the continually expanding population (not to mention the creation of consumer needs through advertising and forced obsolescence). The implications have been that consumer needs are growing too fast to be overtaken by automation-caused unemployment. These arguments describe a trend that has been true to a point, but all trends change and this point is now here. If trends did not change, our civilization would still be that of the anthropoid who had just started to walk upright.

Consider the following dissociated set of facts: We are presently at the point where the rate of population expansion in the nation is slowing down. Other industrial nations, including our enemies of political principle, have been spurting ahead industrially and are capturing increasingly larger portions of the world market. The Soviet bloc, including East Germany, Czechoslovakia, Poland, and Hungary, has been contributing immensely to the cybernetics and automation literature. Khrushchev's boast that the Soviet Union would bury the West was made just prior to the dedication of a national cybernetics institute initially staffed by four to five hundred physical, biological, and behavioral scientists, mathematicians, and educators. Soviet students have been carrying portable teaching machines on their vacations for at least four years. It appears, theoretically, that any process that can be systematized can be cybernated, and processes that appear at first to be subject to nonsystematic contingencies can also be cybernated with the aid of sensors, feedback systems, and appropriate programming. United States industry now has the immediate capability to build and employ inexpensive cybernation. Those new production functions, which are required by cybernation and new products, are themselves subject to cybernation.

These facts, and many others, are the change factors that invalidate historical precedent and linear prediction from trends, that will be responsible for an industrial and cultural revolution having an impact easily surpassing that of the industrial revolution.

APPENDIX

PREDICTED COMPUTER COSTS

We have already given a rough estimate of microelectronic computer costs. However, a closer look at the distribution of computer production costs will provide a better understanding of the relative costs of different types of computers and their associated equipment. Factors in the production cost of a computer system are as follows:

1. The circuitry of the central computer.
2. The memory core.
3. Control/display mechanisms and mechanical structure and cabinetry of the central computer.
4. Peripheral equipment such as tape transports, card punches, card readers, and printers.

Depending on the purpose for which the system is to be used each of the above factors is variable, and depending on the state-of-the-art and other production costs, the cost of any one of the above-mentioned factors may vary. Thus it would be difficult to predict the cost of computer systems accurately. Estimates of a gross nature, however, are possible.

A microelectronic digital logic circuit circa early 1964 cost a hundred to a thousand times less to produce than its equivalent, constructed of discrete solid state components, cost in 1960, most of the 1964 cost being in the packaging. By the summer of 1965, the state-of-the-art had advanced to the point where highly automated mass production and greater integration of functions per circuit had resulted in an even greater reduction of costs, as exemplified by the extremely low cost of IBM's thin film circuits. (Thin film circuits are usually more expensive to produce than integrated semiconductor circuits.) Grossly calculated therefore, the circuitry being utilized in the logic sections and peripheral electronic sections of 1966 computer systems cost in the magnitude of a thousand times less to produce than the equivalent circuit functions for computers produced in 1960. The cost of a central computer (minus memory core and peripheral equipment), however, also includes the cost of the mechanical structure and cabinetry and the various electromechanical control/display mechanisms, these contributing about 10 to 15 per cent of the cost of a 1960 computer. Although microelectronic construction will in itself not have any direct effect on the cost of a computer's electromechanical devices, the large reduction in volume[10] of such construction will require less structure and cabinetry, thereby bringing about a moderate saving. Thus the central computer in any process control or data-processing system will cost hundreds to thousands of times less to produce than the conventional computer.[11]

Because computers have many different applications, requiring many different configurations of associated equipments and systems, the costing of complete systems would be extremely difficult. The associated equipment required to link the controlling computer to manufacturing processes varies even more than the peripheral systems utilized in the various

[10] Microelectronic construction reduces the volume of a computer in two ways. Not only does the circuit function require less space but microelectronic logic circuits operate faster because the current travels a shorter distance. Fewer logic circuits are thus needed as speed of operation can replace circuitry in producing the required number of operations per unit time.

[11] Between 1960 and 1965, the reduction in cost of solid state circuitry had made the magnetic memory core the costliest single item in the system, the magnetic elements and wire network being laboriously hand assembled. Computers that have recently been released to the market now contain thin film memory cores that have brought production costs down by magnitudes equivalent to the cost reduction in circuitry brought about by microelectronics.

multipurpose and specialized data-processing systems. However, a consideration of costing based on a conventional computer system can provide a qualitative understanding of the cost changes that can be expected.

TABLE 2

Cost of a Representative Computer System and Estimated Cost of Circuitry Contained

	Price	Estimated Price of Circuitry
Computer: Including magnetic core storage of 32,768 words, console, typewriter, paper tape reader and punch, motor, generator with controls, instruction books, installation, and checkout.	$1,030,000	$161,500
High Speed Line Printer:	73,500	24,500
Card Reader Controller:	15,500	14,500
Magnetic Tape Controller:	66,000	65,000
Magnetic Disk File Controller:	91,000	90,000
Card Punch Controller:	13,700	12,700
High Speed Card Reader:	22,500	2,000
Magnetic Tape Transport:	36,000	3,000
Magnetic Disk File:	118,000	10,000
Digital Communication Terminal:	24,800	20,800
Data Set Controller:	19,300	18,300
Line Module:	2,400	2,250
TOTALS	$1,512,700	$424,550

Table 2 contains the 1964 catalogue prices of the Control Data Company's (CDC) 1604-A Computer and of the associated peripheral systems that were then available. A number of factors make an accurate analysis of computer cost factors almost impossible. Computer producers do not divulge costing information and no catalogue of computer systems presents cost information in such a way that the separate costs of electronic, electromechanical, and structural components can be determined. In addition, the market price of a computer system does not reflect its production cost as the industry varies substantially in manufacturing methodology and production efficiency. Also, those producers with greater production efficiency and/or resources may be restrained from substantial reduction of prices by the possibility of government antitrust action.

Nevertheless, an order of magnitude calculation of the relative costs of circuitry versus electromechanical devices in computer systems is possible. The third column of Table 2, entitled Estimated Cost of Circuitry, contains an estimate of the cost of the circuitry in the computer and in each peripheral system. The first step in the derivation of these costs was the rough determination of the relative volume of the electromechanical versus electronic content of the computer and each of the peripheral systems. The cost estimates of the electronic portions of the 1604-A Computer and its peripheral systems were then determined by assigning a cost ratio of 10 to 1 by volume for electromechanical devices and electronic circuits respectively.[12]

The totals in Table 2 appear to indicate that electronic circuitry accounts for approximately one-third of the total price of the 1604-A Computer and its full range of peripheral systems ($424,550). Microelectronics would reduce the cost of the circuitry in the 1604-A complex by an approximate factor of a thousand (to $424.55). If we assume the reduction in the price of magnetic memory cores, brought about by thin film technology, to be the same as the reductions in circuit costs that were brought about by microelectronics, we must also reduce the memory core price by a factor of a thousand. Thus, as the memory core contributes an estimated 70 per cent to the price of the central computer ($728,000), a thin film memory core will cost $728. Therefore, if we substitute the reduced price of central computer circuitry and

[12] The rough determination of relative volume was done by Herman Englander of the Navy Electronics Laboratory, a computer design expert. The 1604-A Computer was selected for cost analysis because it is a representative computer used for scientific data processing. The 10 to 1 cost ratio is a rule of thumb used in rough engineering estimates for the contemporary states-of-the-art in electromechanical devices and pre-microelectronic solid state circuitry.

memory core ($1,153) for the estimated 1964 circuitry and memory core price ($889,000), we find that the price of the central computer has been reduced from $1,030,000 to $141,143). The price of the total computer complex is reduced from $1,512,700 to $360,150.

Other considerations relative to the initial cost of computers are

1. The type of computer complex required for the purpose.
2. Progress in electronic and electromechanical devices.
3. Automation of computer and component production.
4. The threat of government antitrust actions.
5. The status of competition.

Relative to the first consideration, the central computer listed in Table 2 contains a magnetic memory core and a number of basic auxiliary equipments that account for about three-quarters of its total price. In addition another half million dollars' worth of peripheral systems is available. Such an installation is still classified as a large multipurpose scientific complex, although higher capacity systems are on the market. However, the great majority of computer systems required by government, industry, and commerce will be for special purposes such as industrial process controls, military systems, and specialized data processing for relatively moderate or small requirements. Such specialized systems generally require fewer auxiliary equipments and peripheral systems of the type included in the calculations above and tend to contain a larger ratio of circuitry to electromechanical devices. The cost reduction attributable to microelectronic circuitry in such specialized computer systems will therefore be much greater.

Relative to the second consideration, constant progress is being made in either replacing electromechanical devices with electronic ones or designing around the need for them. Some instances of this are the replacement of the rotating machinery in analogue systems with digital design, the replacement of relays with transistors, the use of heat- and pressure-sensitive solid state electronic devices to replace those of more complex mechanical construction, and the replacement of electromechanically driven potentiometers with transistorized voltage ladders. The 10 to 1 cost reduction ratio applicable to the replacement of contemporary electromechanical devices with electronic devices or circuits can become even more favorable (possibly a ratio of 10,000 or more to 1) through the use of improved microelectronic and other solid state techniques.

In respect to the third consideration, it is to be expected that the automation industry will be foremost among the automated industries. IBM has been using computers to build computers for some time now. As refinements are made in automated production methods, even small batches of high precision electromechanical devices will be produced at low cost, driving the production and testing costs of office, scientific, and industrial cybernation systems down by substantial amounts.

Relative to the fourth and fifth consideration, IBM in 1965 was responsible for approximately 85 per cent of the nation's computer production, and only two other United States producers were selling computers on the open market at a profit. Other producers were corporate divisions that were maintained by their parent corporations though not showing a profit. Thus, if IBM were to market computers at a price sufficiently low to drive out competition, it could be faced by federal antitrust action. The utilization of microelectronic techniques will now enable price cuts to originate with the smaller producers, thereby allowing major price competition for the first time in the history of the computer industry.

To summarize, the likelihood of steep reductions in computer prices results from the thousandfold decrease in the cost of computer circuitry and magnetic memory cores; the prospect of the replacement of an undetermined amount of expensive (and less reliable) electromechanical devices with circuitry and solid state devices that would further greatly reduce the cost per function; the automation of computer system production, including the production of electromechanical devices; and the establishment of competitive pricing of computers. The production costs of early microelectronic computer systems should be reduced by a minimum of one-quarter of the 1964 costs if they contain many electromechanical and magnetic memory core devices (as per the multipurpose CDC 1604-A), and in the magnitude of close to a thousandfold if they contain little or no electromechanical content. Further progress in the elimination of expensive components, in production efficiency, and in open market competition should drive the market prices of computers downward even further within the next few years.

SECOND-ORDER COMMITTED SPENDING: THE SUPPORT OF INNOVATION

R. Christian Anderson

The time is not far off when certain forms of minimal economic security will be universally available in technological societies. Such security, by whatever name, will be dictated by the growing sense of social justice and by the need for, as well as the possibility of, the more equitable distribution of that wealth that technological rather than human energy produces. This sort of capital is not convertible into all the needs of man. But the call for the general and unconditional provision of the necessities of life is unmistakable. The way is open to the higher order needs of man.

The rearrangement of values whereby material abundance is put at the disposal of the larger dimensions of life will require a concerted effort. It will require action of the state as the principal entity external to the industrial economy. Government spending must be committed to renewal, scholarship, research, aesthetic appreciation as well as to ensure equity, maintain an aggregate demand for goods, provide for the national security. It must commit spending to those individuals and institutions that are responsible for our present advancement and put them to the wider task of reasserting the superior claims of other than economic goals.

If the aims of an industrial system are being fairly met, if movements are afoot to reduce the inequities and excesses a democracy must not condone, the time has come to begin a new social order. We need not fear that in such an order the release of men from the burden of seeking material requirements will lead to nothing but unproductive leisure. Man will want to remain occupied. It is with the nature, quality, and pace of that occupation that we must become concerned.

Before turning directly to this issue, it might be well to suggest why it may be of crucial importance. Proposals designed to reduce modern man's preoccupation with the values of a predominately materialistic culture face several difficulties. If we argue as Bacon argued three hundred years ago that science should be put to the task of the relief of man's estate, and further, that our new-found technological strength —new found because science has transformed our older industrial strength—is now sufficient to the task, the resistance to guaranteed annual incomes resides principally in ideologies no longer viable. The work ethic of the Western world must give way if it stands, as it does, in the way of social justice. The transition from an economy of scarcity to one of affluence alters the priorities. Economic as well as social democracy cannot be denied much longer.

By and large, the now orthodox devices of government for Committed Spending, such as public works, monetary control, subsidies, social security, are internal to an industrial economy. They are employed to provide stability and promote growth of that economy. They reflect standards of cost consciousness, efficiency, and the desire to maintain the general features of corporate capitalism. But as necessary as these devices may be, they cannot but result in an insufficient amount of spending for constructive refreshment of our intellectual and artistic resources or the conservation or replenishment of our natural resources.

No little part of this pattern of spending reflects the fact that the political system responds to the quantity of power it meets, either the statistical weight of the electorate, or the financial resources of concerted special interest groups. A system of checks and balances seldom can, in itself, be the leading source of innovation.

Further, the fact that the industrial and business community is, or appears to be, self-contained and that the body public is concerned with manifestations of concerted power contribute directly to the resistance that greets efforts to spend for quality, enlightenment, or aesthetic goals. Intelligence and sensitivity, being difficult to subvert, are suspect and cannot be allowed complete freedom, not to mention any considerable amount of support. Here again, the influence of science may begin to be felt; for the first time arguments can be made that our collective affluence is increasingly, perhaps critically, due to the direct use of man's power to reason in this particular way.

It is no longer possible to ensure our well-being just with capital and invention, with exploitation and expansion. The probability of any decent advance, including a proper and desirable increase of the industrial strength that exists, now turns on the questions of understanding and maintaining the support of well-educated, creative, gifted individuals. It would be repugnant to ask for support of them either as individuals or a class, but the fact remains that tempered, unfettered intelligence will be required to help resolve some of the dilemmas of our age, which have been created by our curiosity, our will to power, our possessiveness.

Our attention is thus drawn to second-order Committed Spending—the policies by which the innovative process is nurtured, the seeds for higher forms of social order are sown.

* * *

Industrialization depended first on the introduction of machines consciously developed to save manual labor and to fill obvious, immediate needs. For the most part they were created by empirical and isolated inventors. Little engineering and less science went into their design. This activity, the improvisation of tools and manual aids, remains the first step in moving from an agricultural to an industrial society. At this state of development, science seems unnecessary and has little effect. Apparently it is only out of acquaintanceship with this first phase of the transformation to an industrial state that a country can develop the climate in which to exploit the fruits of science. Sophisticated technology cannot for this reason be directly transplanted at will to any alien culture. Before science becomes an economic force there must exist workers familiar with the simpler industrial techniques; there must be systematic education of large numbers of the young; there must be a nexus of sophisticated ideas politicians can use and economists exploit. The next step, the development of technology based on science, cannot be traced so easily. For one thing, crucial and entirely new elements came out of a tradition long separated from the main currents of agriculture, commerce, or industry. It is to be found in the scientific tradition. This tradition in turn must be seen for its contrast to the mainstreams of intellectual activity in the last four hundred years. Science is to a certain degree antirational. It is tuned as much to pragmatic curiosity about the world as to the embellishment of a particular philosophic vision. The main features of this achievement of man include a belief in the existence of order, symmetry, and regularity in the natural world and faith in the ability of man to discover and examine that order. It includes the appearance of a special ingenuity—the invention of scientific instruments. The need for devices to test ideas has helped form the bridge to the concurrent but originally separate tradition of practical invention. The rationale of science is to test ideas by the use, in powerful conjunction, of a set of theoretical models and instruments designed to test these models. The goal remains the attainment of new knowledge, new understanding, and only peripherally new techniques and practical applications.

It is preeminently an intellectual activity, requiring a massive investment in education and mental apprenticeship. The values include commitment to the evidence and objectivity in analyzing the results of the interplay of theory and experiment. The output is a patient accretion of verified information freely disseminated. It is a tradition based on the desire to know, not a need to know. The creation of nuclear reactors, electronic computers, weather satellites, and a host of other modern tools arises out of the efforts of scientists. It is almost inconceivable that they would have been discovered through trial and error invention.

As often as not, the original search for scientific knowledge had no connection with the application finally made of that knowledge. This disengagement exists not only between the immediate product of the innovator and the social or economic use to which it is ultimately put, but also between the innovator and the means of his support. Research is but loosely coupled with the aims and values of the surrounding society. It cannot be organized from the outside. Numbers of men or quantities of money cannot substitute for the intellectual daring, courage, and genius of individuals. But it is also true that scientists do not operate in a cultural or historical vacuum; they are not prophets or divines separate from organized society. Their thrust into new intellectual realms occurs while they are active elements in the matrix of their own time. It would be a mistake, therefore, to assume that no coupling exists at all. The physicist, for example, is the product of a distinct cultural heritage, which mirrors the general interests of the intellectual community of his age. That Aristotle was interested in fishes, the manifold forms of life, or Newton in optics, or, for that matter, Fermi in neutrons, is not fortuitous. Each of these great innovators benefited from the collective genius and nascent ideas of their own time.

The practical link between the scientist and society has been the patron. But the simple, spontaneous, intimate relationship that once existed has been replaced by a complex, formal, social structure in which the scientist is separated from his new patron, the taxpayer, by government, agency, institution, administration. The Renaissance patron has given way to organizations, some corporate, some governmental, some, in more recent times, academic.

Research has finally become an accustomed part of the

university, so that today they seem inseparable and, as with a couple grown old together, have begun to look like each other. It is part of the conventional wisdom to assume the role of research and education has always been close and in harmony. However, certain of the things sacrificed in their union were valuable and worth regaining. The patron gave early science a special freedom, an autonomy bred of mutual respect and understanding. When research became a part of the university, at least in the United States, the support was strongly marked by a sense of public service, as, for example, was spelled out in and resulted from the land grant act sponsored by Morrill. Concurrently, the university turned from its traditional last to try its hand at service in external fields with the loss of autonomy and flexibility. The independence so necessary for the critical faculty of scholarship to operate in leisure and at a decent pace has begun to give way.

Several important features emerge from an examination of the scientific tradition. The characteristics of the men mentioned above, of being fully aware but gently disengaged, are an essential feature of any culture, any social system that depends, as does ours, on innovation for its vigor. It also speaks for the autonomy of institutions that serve the innovators' needs, whether universities or research institutions. It suggests that conditions permitting such men to be freely creative can serve as models for their extension to other members of the community who determine values and influence opinion. It also underlines the difficulties in attempting to jump from an agricultural to a "cybernated" society. The leap needs more than technique, it requires a cultural transformation.

* * *

The principal function of a plan for economic security, at least as regards the innovators in the society, would be to release them from subordination to work policies and patterns designed for an entirely different purpose—the efficient use of machines. The most conspicuous feature of the modern industrial society is the imposition of regular work patterns. Men are required to be at certain stations, performing certain duties within certain hours, no matter the phase of the moon, the quality of the sunlight, the smell of the open meadow or deep wood. These fixed hours grow into fixed work weeks, fixed years, and a specified portion of a man's lifetime. It is assumed, when he enters this Procrustean bed, that he is educated enough for the purposes of his employer, and will need no more. It is also assumed that his productivity is constant throughout his working career. When he reaches a certain age he is retired whether spent or not. Coming from another planet one might not be surprised to see certain groups of workers, so inclined and prepared, to be so engaged, but astonished to find this work pattern affecting almost everyone touched by the industrial system. One must grant that certain formal relations, some special commitment must exist between worker and the demands of an industrial society. But that this be applied to those individuals employed for their minds, no matter their milieu, is indefensible.

At the present time the most liberal conditions under which an intellectual may be employed is in a university. Typically his career begins at the age of twenty-eight, after receiving a doctorate at twenty-six and spending two years as a postdoctoral fellow. He will, if he has talent and works hard, attain a tenure position in his early thirties and will then qualify for periodic leaves at intervals of about six years, each leave being something less than a year in duration. Then he is retired, usually not before or very much after he reaches the age of sixty-five. He finds that to earn a sufficient income to travel and to reinvest, through his children's education, in maintaining the quality of his part of the culture, that he has to work summers, usually on government funds for which reports of progress must be made and renewals solicited. He also sees that the periodic leave is hedged with conditions, such as whether his department can spare him, that little or no travel money is available, that by the time he qualifies, his children's schooling cannot be interrupted. Finally, he is retired at an age that has nothing to do with his vigor, or lack of it, but the prevailing economic conditions and the state of his annuity. At retirement he may or may not retain the privilege of an office or access to library or laboratory facilities.

Even under the best of conditions this pattern would not be entirely satisfactory. It has become increasingly intolerable as the universities have traded their autonomy for the dubious role of direct public service. It makes little sense, that, as education for enlightenment and the search for beauty become imperatives, the educational apparatus takes on, to an uncomfortable degree, the characteristics of modern technological industry.

This recital records nothing of the growing daily pressures that exist even in this apparently relaxed pattern of work. Contact hours, study loads, the paperwork and reports give the lie to a picture of scholarly leisure.

The competitive spirit of the marketplace has invaded the university and research institution. The cost accounting practices of business are thought appropriate to the instruments of science, the pursuit of research and scholarship. Faculty members are chosen on the basis of their ability to bring in outside contracts. The demand for talent to fulfill the universities' least important but more expensive function of public service generates a climate of frenzy, worldliness, and mediocrity. Public funds are being used, under increasingly restrictive conditions, to expand staffs, introduce accounting practices, establish personnel policies, and effectively industrialize the groves of academe. No one can deny that these developments reveal a strong paradox. While a sophisticated technology is moving to ease the burden of the vast proportion of individuals in advanced countries, intolerable pressures are being applied to that realm of activities and those who have made the discoveries basic to that very technology.

It is clearly necessary to stop or reverse the trend toward further regimentation of educated and educator alike, intellectuals in general whether part of organizations or not. Education and the concomitant output of new ideas, refinement of values, artistic and musical creativity, must be recognized as a high service. Freedom from obsolete or inappropriate work patterns would seem to be a perfectly sound reason for introducing substantial second order economic security for creative individuals in a progressive democracy.

* * *

If decent conditions of occupation are to be reestablished in any institution that employs workers whose value lies in their creative capacities, liberal arrangements for continual education and refreshment, for leaves for professional advancement, as well as a completely revised system of annuities must be instituted.

As for continuing education, various possibilities exist. In industrial laboratories it might consist of annual two- to four-week study leaves for those in mentally demanding jobs. Such leaves need not be hedged by formal attendance at the university. This only increases rather than lessens the current burden on educational institutions. This would be hardly more than the time now spent serving in the military reserve. For university staff it would involve adequate summer grants to travel and to work at other than the home institution, without the necessity of engaging in the business of the world via an outside project or contract.

Leaves for intellectual refreshment should become as common as such fringe benefits as vacation, sick leave, and retirement annuities. Such leave should be vested, carry not only salary but adequate travel allowances, and should be available from the beginning of an individual's career and independent of the nature of his long-term affiliation. As matters stand, sabbatical leaves in most institutions come too late and cannot be efficiently used. It is not Utopian to suppose that senior post-doctoral fellowships sponsored by the federal government could be extended to cover this sort of activity. Here is an existing mechanism that, if sufficiently expanded, would suit as a means of Committed Spending with a relatively large social and economic effect in the long run. Again, this is second-order spending since it is on top of the basic allowance and granted for demonstrated creativity.

Finally, an arrangement must be found to promote mobility among scholars, artists, writers, and research workers. It should be possible to offer, and indeed may at some point be necessary to offer, bonuses to individuals to move on to new situations at or near mid-career. This mechanism exists in a reverse form by virtue of the scarcity of top-flight people, in that universities and laboratories offer premium salaries to attract them away from their own institutions. The difficulty with this, however, is that it distorts the balance between favored institutions and those that must be supported in any event, such as regional universities or liberal arts colleges that cannot compete directly. A large reserve of very good people would become available to the multitude of young, rapidly growing institutions still lacking in standards and quality if early and adequate pensions were available. The use, but not the magnitude of civil and military service pensions, serves as an illustration of what might be done to encourage mobility and take advantage of the desire to change pace and milieu.

Whether the pension is incorporated in the salary at the new institution (paid by the government via grants) or treated as a vested annuity earned at the old institution will need to be examined carefully.

Early mobility, as contrasted to retirement, annuities would allow the innovator whose creative pace has slowed the opportunity to teach in institutions where full-time research is not possible or encouraged for its own sake, and at the same time make available to those institutions experienced faculty at an acceptable cost, without upsetting the consistency of its salary scales.

It would afford the still strong innovator the opportunity to change the direction of his interests which, though always possible, is seldom practical at one institution. Whether teaching or doing research, the individual becomes identified with a particular department or program and may find it impossible to break the rhythm of his commitments.

It would give institutions with but a single function, such as scientific research, the possibility of high turnover of staff. For not only is the creative impulse of individuals of finite duration, the rate of change in knowledge and techniques makes the concept of a permanent staff in intellectually active institutions an anachronism. Science and the institutions in which it has been practiced have enjoyed a long period of uninterrupted exponential growth. But this is coming to an end. Since research laboratories now must maintain their vitality with relatively stable resources, no longer depending on that rate of growth for their momentum, the rate of change of staff and facilities within the limits of the resources must be sharply increased.

The availability of a mobility pension or annuity might also play a part in solving the vexing problem of early retirement. The rate of change in many fields is so great as to leave many workers unable to keep up no matter what techniques of recreation are employed. Some individuals may wish to retire from active work late, some early. The device of a mobility pension effective before the age when normal social security is available would in many cases be the least expensive alternative open to an institution. A little courage on the part of academic and research administrations and granting agencies in recognizing this is needed, but so is the provision of a great deal more autonomy to the institutions that must deal with the problem.

These various proposals for increasing creativity without greatly increasing the number of active participants and thus avoiding unduly high and unrealistic rates of growth may be illustrated as follows:

The fresh university graduate who does not elect to follow a profession but enter corporate, private, or civil service might anticipate the following alternatives. He could do research for two years just after obtaining the highest available academic degree on a current problem in his field in one of a number of institutions while unhampered by the formal requirements that to this point marked his apprenticeship. He would then go to a research institution, industrial laboratory, or university, where the opportunity every year of a short educational leave to attend formal courses or simply study while on full pay and with tuition reimbursed would be available. In five to seven years he could take up to a year's leave to study, do research elsewhere, or accept public service, such as government duty or in a post in a foreign country teaching or even, perish the thought, doing nothing. At this point in his career, our worker is about thirty-three to thirty-five years old, his children are not yet in high school, and he can move with relative ease.

His next extended leave would be available to him in his early forties, say after fifteen to twenty years of service to his institution. Should he prove as vigorous as ever, be at the forefront of a field of endeavor still a major pursuit of the institution, he would take another year's leave and return. But should his interest in research wane, or other fields beckon to him, or the institution itself take a divergent direction, he should be able to make a change that would not seriously jeopardize his existing standard of living or his retirement annuity. The new position might be teaching at a small school, in administration, in foreign service, in an industrial laboratory, in a governmental agency. In any event, he would receive payments that would make up some part of the difference between his new and old salary, but with a guarantee at some level of income. The payments would be adjusted so as to encourage him to maintain an affiliation with an institution and would reflect his standing at the time he went on leave. The amount of salary would be a function of his productivity to that date. Indeed, should it be clearly in his interests to do so, he could retire without fearing the consequences of a reduction to a bare maintenance income. However, it would be unlikely as the transition to a post-industrial age takes place that the highly educated individual would not find a suitable position. A number of innovators early in their careers would make excellent teachers later on, but not if they must wait as now until retirement at sixty or sixty-five years of age. A mobility pension would allow the change at a much better time for both the individual and institution.

The advantages of some form of mobility payments are manifold. They must soon be considered a legitimate part of the cost of doing business and maintaining sensible standards, whether in public or private institutions.

* * *

It is not, however, possible to rely only on the extension of existing policies or the creation of new programs designed to gain maximum creativity from individuals in whom a heavy educational investment has been made. Making such leaves and annuities available at existing institutions, valuable though that would be, will not be sufficient. New institutions need be chartered. In certain isolated cases, institutions already exist that could form the nucleus of these organizations. For them it would be a matter of rehabilitation.

To complement the present range of academic and research organizations, new institutes of advanced study should be created. These should be seen not only as different from the rehabilitation of existing universities by identifying them as new centers of excellence, but in many instances as substitutes for such a scheme. The strains and tensions inherent in the educational system up to the level of predoctoral studies are evident enough. Force-feeding institutions that are growing rapidly in student enrollment to broaden the scope of their structure further will only increase the distress.

The formation of new organizations in a hitherto almost vacant level of intellectual activity has much to recommend it. Such high-level institutions would serve many purposes, not the least of which would be to redress the several imbalances that have been introduced by the demands of scientific and applied research on the traditional academic institution.

A typical advanced institute might be governed by a national board of trustees, supported by the federal government under a grant rather than a cost reimbursement contract and free of any direct affiliations with other existing establishments. The board of trustees would be chosen from among the peers of those who would work in the institute, and not necessarily those chosen for their accomplishments in other fields of endeavor. Lay boards may very well serve the needs of institutions more closely aligned to the more immediate needs of society, but the control of the high-level organizations envisaged here must rest with those with the most advanced training and demonstrated ability.

The use of grants as against cost reimbursement contracts would seem obvious in the light of the arguments for decoupling the patron and the innovator. Each institute might have a resident staff numbering at any one time no more than a quarter to a third of the authorized full-time complement of staff. The remainder of the staff would consist of post-doctoral fellows, occasional members, and senior research associates. The latter would be those very individuals enjoying a leave for professional advancement, or an educational refreshment period; individuals who are in mid-career, and who may return to teaching or leave teaching; or those who may wish to prepare for a second career. Further, those individuals who by virtue of their interests or talents move at the edge of the intellectual community could be accommodated in a flexible way. The administrative and technical support would vary according to the nature of the facilities provided. The former can in any case be small since the institute's operation is predicated on a high degree of autonomy. This would be in distinct contrast to the present enervating, time- and money-consuming procedures dictated by agencies that are obliged to account for and, therefore, wish to manage the sources of federal funds. The corps of technical assistants in the institutes will be a function of how much experimental equipment is required. Indeed, it is important to separate the provision and maintenance of equipment from questions of staff size. The artificial division of certain kinds of physics into big and little is due to the size and complexity of equipment, not necessarily to the volume of brains put to the task at hand.

In any given institute emphasis would be placed on several areas of scholarship and research. Under no circumstances, however, could these areas be restricted to either what are now labeled scientific disciplines on the one hand, or humanistic on the other. The reestablishment of easy and active dialogue within the entire house of intellect is long overdue. In the universities this dialogue has begun to suffer because of the growing primacy of the function of increasingly pedestrian teaching of more and more professionally oriented courses. And to a degree these new institutes must be self-serving, it being realized that in such service to the intellectual community the general good may be advanced.

The contribution to education in these organizations would not be unimportant. Since, as has been argued, education of innovators will be continual, the conditions under which this is accomplished must vary with the age of the students. This, in itself, would suggest a spectrum of institutions, each with a different mixture of formal teaching and unregulated scholarship. The view that teaching and research are inseparable is true if one thinks of teaching as a process of learning for the teacher. The degree to which the teacher and student are an intellectual match and have not too disparate backgrounds determines whether the combination is necessary or productive. Post-doctoral institutes do have an educational function—one that is too little recognized and exploited. At such institutes, given the proper means of support and enlightened administration, the need for certain ancient guarantees of freedom, embodied in the concept of tenure, would tend to disappear. If economic security exists and autonomy is protected, freedom of expression need not be in jeopardy. Should, however, a given institute become exhausted—such an eventuality must be anticipated if mediocrity or mismanagement is to be avoided—it should be disbanded and its constituent staff given mobility or early retirement annuities. The cost of such pensions are demonstrably cheaper than keeping an obsolete institution going. If we write off investments in business adventures with the aid of government, we must be prepared to do so in any publicly supported institution.

A number of exciting combinations could be established in these institutes—which will then serve enormously to stimulate the movement to new and productive areas of human activities. The institutes in which medical research was supported might invest in ethics. Mathematics might coexist with literature, philosophy with physics, engineering with aesthetics. Institutes could become international in character and the temporary ebb and flow of talented individuals between countries come in time to be accepted as normal, healthy, and desirable.

The proposal for senior institutions may be viewed as the rehabilitation of the concept of a federal university so long dreamed of in the United States. The essential new idea in regard to such an institution, which now would have to be in many separate installations, is that it would not compete with the present structure of schools, colleges, and universities but provide the means for extending opportunities for education, reflection, and scholarship well beyond those available in institutions granting academic and professional degrees. Perhaps these various institutes could be loosely coupled under a federation, thus enabling an exchange of staff among the constituent institutes, as well as in and out of the federation. The political difficulties in seeking economic support to maintain innovation would be considerably eased when that support could be shown to issue through such an institutional framework.

The case for Committed Spending is manifold. The wealth of a technological economy must be spent in various ways, since equity must be balanced against the need to create and to establish high orders of values. To free man from the machine, to reintroduce the idea of true leisure, to guarantee freedom of pace and action by larger numbers of individuals in an energy and capital-rich society should become reasonable expectations. High-order Committed Spending already exists, but the expressed reasons for it must be recast. Science could, once again, be supported for the intellectual adventure and ornament it is and not, as now, as a handmaiden to war and industry. Society might enjoy afresh the excitement of a commonwealth of learning, one embracing scholars, peripatetic teachers, and students of all ages and disciplines. The choice of commitment and possibility of social dignity might be open to every man.

EFFECT ON ARTISTIC ACTIVITY

George Nelson

The title of this paper contains an implied question: in what way are people engaged in "artistic" pursuits different from other people? "Prick me," said Shylock, "and I bleed." Obviously this is not the kind of difference we are looking for. But the meaning of money, for Shylock, was different from the meaning to his customers. Is a guaranteed income different for the painter and the plumber? If it is, what exactly *is* the difference? There are myths about artists and other kinds of creative people: it is said that they are not highly motivated by money. Are plumbers more likely to be seduced by it?

The guaranteed income is the Siamese twin of exploding cybernation. Without the latter there is no point in schemes for distributing abundance to involuntary non-producers so that they may become more active consumers. Turning the coin, then (and mixing the metaphor at the same time) will the painter be more or less affected by cybernation than the plumber? Directly, or indirectly? Is it possible that the Henry Moores and the Braques of this world are destined to go the way of Mr. Kaplan's TV repairman? If so, there will be less rejoicing, for nobody loves a TV repairman. We know the difference between the artist and the repairman. But what are the differences between artists and others who are also concerned with aesthetic problems? Everyone knows, or thinks he knows, what an artist is. An artist is someone who creates useless beauty. A leaky roof cannot be repaired with a painting, and you cannot mow a lawn with a piece of sculpture. These are beautiful things, but only to be looked at. Or perhaps not so beautiful in your or my eyes. But we must be careful here, for if we openly judge the new art to be ugly, our children will deride us as hopeless squares. Art is for museums, art galleries, and rich collectors. The role of the public is to flock to see it, to try earnestly to understand, to struggle to upgrade its level of understanding and taste. Painters, sculptors, and the like are artists; we are all agreed on this. But what about designers?

Designers are people who create hats, dresses, automobile bodies, packages, airplane interiors, and the look of most consumer products. Is this work artistic, or is it something else? For the purposes of this paper I am going to assume that since the work of such people is largely concerned with the appearance of things, and since each in his way is attempting to create beauty of a sort, we are justified in tossing them into the same pot as the artist, although they aren't really the same breed of cat at all. For similar reasons we might as well include the architects, specialized designers of buildings, for the more conscientious members of this ancient and occasionally noble profession certainly try to do more for their clients than keep out the weather. Most of the tourist magnets in most countries are buildings of one sort or another.

Beyond these groups, already sizable in most developed countries, the "artistic" component becomes increasingly difficult to isolate. There are large structures—bridges, dams, old fortifications—that are widely held to be objects of surpassing beauty, and yet one does not think of the engineer as one whose primary concern is aesthetic content. Such works as the Brooklyn Bridge, or the magnificent bridge over the river Forth, or the Roman aqueduct in Segovia are truly lovely things, but one persists nonetheless in thinking of the engineer as a non-artist. If he does come up with something of unexpected beauty, we regard this as a plus, a bonus, for he was hired to design a structure that would not collapse. For these reasons, I think we had better pass by the engineer and leave him for someone else to deal with, admirable though he and his works may be.

I have left the craftsmen as a group apart, for many of

them are not professionals at all, and the purpose of craft activity is not a sharply defined thing, like the designing of hats or civic monuments. The crafts are used, for instance, to tranquilize small children and the inmates of lunatic asylums. They also provide occupational therapy for convalescents and the physically handicapped. They sometimes serve as hobbies—escape mechanisms—for people who feel somewhat submerged in the modern world or who, quite simply, hate what they have to do to earn a living. There are part-time craftsmen, like the Sunday painters, and there are full-time pros who earn their livelihood with their work. There are craftsmen who are first-rate artists, but who are set apart from, say, the painters, because their creations can be walked on, worn, or otherwise used. The craft people, despite the mixed motives that animate them as a group, definitely deserve a place here if we omit a few of the objectives like therapy. The craftsmen, as I have already suggested, can be distinguished from the "pure" artists because of the functional nature of their output. They are also identified by their persistent use of archaic and primitive techniques for making things. One thinks of a craftsman as someone who makes wood furniture by hand, or who throws pots on a wheel, or weaves, or makes jewelry. Should the success of his designs put him into production, he is no longer a craftsman, but a manufacturer. We expect one-of-a-kind things from the crafts, or at the very outside, a production sharply limited by handwork and simple tools.

We now have three main groups conveniently lumped under the banner of "artistic" activity—artists, designers, and craftsmen—and while the boundaries between them are anything but stable, there are enough significant differences for us to treat them as separate. We are concerned with the effect of a guaranteed income on their working lives and it is also interesting to consider in what ways they might be affected by the galloping advance of cybernation. My impression is that these effects might be quite different in each of the three groups.

The public image of the artist today is still to a large extent the Victorian image: he is an oddball, a nonconformist in dress and behavior, he lives in lofts or garrets by preference, and his interest in money is confined to its use for survival. In the post-war years the image has faded somewhat. Both the press and the public view the work of contemporary artists with uneasy respect, if only because of the prices their work brings these days. I know at least two artists whose fleets of personal cars include vehicles by Rolls Royce, and one suspects that Picasso and Chagall could match J. Paul Getty's annual income if they felt like trying. However, the mass of artists, like the mass of grocery clerks, are not especially well off, and a monthly check out of Washington would probably look like manna from heaven. I am not sure that the spending of the artists would give as much joy to U.S. industry as the spending of the clerks, whose interest in shiny, status-type gadgetry is more predictable. The effect of a degree of financial security would be greatest, I think, on the mass of artists (or would-be artists) who now live on the fringe of the activity they like best while grinding out a supplementary subsistence income through some form of moonlighting. The educational institutions are full of such people—for example, painters who would prefer painting to teaching. For these, a reliable income, even though small, might enable them to make the switch to the work they prefer. It wouldn't take too much. There is actually a sizable group of the young these days (California seems to have the highest concentration) who manage to avoid all forms of gainful employment through combinations of unemployment compensation, communal living, and an occasional foundation grant. True, the majority of these probably have no dedication to the arts, but the point is that it *can* be done, and most young artists are familiar with the tricks of evading what used to be called "social responsibility," that is, respectable employment. If the computers and automation do to employment what so many predict, the same behavior will then be viewed, in all probability, as heroic.

There are other aspects of the present-day artist's stance vis-à-vis his society that come into the picture. There is a great deal of bafflement today regarding the meaning of what the artists are doing, and only the critics have the courage to pretend that they understand everything that is going on. This general confusion has led to a flourishing of quackery on a truly monumental scale, for few dare to suggest that the king may have no clothes on. But through all the work, fake or for real, there runs a pretty consistent and visible thread: the artists, by and large, take less than a rosy view of the society to which they are showing their wares. Pop art, for instance, selects the most vulgar aspects of the society as its subject matter. It displays no belief in anything, no real admiration of anything, not even liking for anything. If art is indeed a mirror of social realities, pop art is vital and shocking in what it shows us; however, its exquisitely sick-making qualities are not to be blamed on the artists, but on the scene itself. Op Art shows another facet: in the laborious executing of complex mechanical patterns, the artists are creating a simulacrum of what the computer hitched to a plotting machine can do. Indeed, these devices have already been programmed to produce material indistinguishable from some op art. The sculptor who signs his name to a cube of metal which was a Buick body before the wrecking yard press got to it, quite clearly has no interest in glorifying the achievements of Detroit's engineers and stylists. The list is far from complete, but I trust that the point is clear: if the artists with such attitudes—and their names are legion—were given some degree of financial security, it seems most unlikely that they would refrain from biting the hand that fed them, and it is almost certain that their numbers would be swelled by desertions from the offices of graphic designers, advertising agencies, and the like, where many artists who would prefer trying to do more meaningful things presently work out of necessity.

As I see it, a proliferation of negators, rejectors, and the generally ungrateful would be all to the good, for we are all but suffocating in the flood of verbal and visual garbage released hourly into the social bloodstream by those whose job it is to glorify the least glorious aspects of our common existence.

Regarding the artist and his relationship to the computer, I find it impossible to believe that he will act out the role of victim. Artists, for all their advertised impracticality, have fantastic survival capabilities. There are even artists in Soviet Russia, something that on the face of it is a logical impossibility. The modern painters and sculptors have already demonstrated with both force and clarity that for them the great onrush of technology is neither menace nor blessing, but another interesting phenomenon to be exploited. The entire inventory of new materials has been assimilated—plastic, stainless steels, light metals, and all the rest of it. There are still painters who paint with brushes and oils, but only because they find it convenient. In other words, the artist is not trapped by tradition, not menaced by the machine, not running out of subject matter. He is not even wedded to the old "one-of-a-kind" attitude—Andy Warhol makes his "paintings" using silk screen reproductions and proudly points out that his work is "untouched by human hands." These parodies and exploitations of the technological process are simply a new device for making statements about the nature of the world as seen by the artist. Thus there is no way of making him a victim of technological unemployment. In fact there is no way of making him unemployed, if he happens to feel like working.

When we come to the designers—I am thinking primarily of industrial, graphic, fashion designers, and architects—the story is quite different. These aesthetically oriented trades show little of the freedom exhibited by the artist, for they are all essentially *service* occupations. An architect cannot function if no one wants his buildings. He must have a client, a customer. I realize that this statement is not 100 per cent true: Le Corbusier put down his dreams for years without clients, Piranesi's famous prisons were never built and Frank Lloyd Wright made many designs that were statements rather than actual building projects. These exceptional people are the rarest of birds, however, and statistically they are invisible. The typical designer waits until he can snare a client, and then designs what the client wants—or needs—and can afford. Money is a big thing in the lives of all designers, not so much in the sense of money for themselves, but because money governs what they can do. An architect who wants to design a one-hundred story tower will remain eternally frustrated if his clients all want elementary schools and an occasional house. The artist is not similarly hampered—as far as money goes, the production cost of the Mona Lisa could not have been much different from Dwight Eisenhower's bill for canvas and paint. Thus the designer is either employed or unemployed. If he is employed, he lives reasonably decently, for the pay scales are good. If he is unemployed, he is in the same bind as anyone else with a family and no job. The great virtue of Committed Spending for such people, I suspect, is that the possibility of an occasional sabbatical leave becomes very real, and it could be most welcome. The stimulation of new sights, people, and ideas is important for individuals who see themselves as creative. The fact that a background of financial security tends to make a person more relaxed may be of particular value to designers, but I doubt it. It is difficult to imagine anyone who would not respond in the same way.

In most of the books and articles that deal with automation, the computer and their influence, it is generally taken for granted that the greatest economic advantages are to be found in such areas as inventory control, accounting, payroll handling, cost reduction, warehousing, general communications, and data retrieval. In such lists—in my own reading, at least—there seems to be an assumption that the so-called "creative" activities would remain outside the direct influence of these devices. Recent developments suggest that this view is a bit on the rosy side, and to come to a clearer picture it is necessary to find out exactly *what is creative* in the creative professions. What we discover rather quickly is that very, very little of all the time and labor expended qualifies as "creative" in any sense at all, and that in actuality the design professions are not at all unlike the scientific disciplines if viewed in the light of the question of what is, or is not, creative. In the sciences there have been creative moments of immense significance, but these are as milliseconds when compared to the work surrounding the creative act. The standard picture in the sciences always presents an immense amount of preliminary labor—measuring, comparing, collecting, checking. At some moment in the process a genuinely creative mind assesses the information and senses an unsuspected meaning which is then presented as a hypothesis. This inspired hunch is then followed by great quantities of uninspired labor designed to verify or disprove the hypothesis. Exactly the same thing holds true in architecture and the other fields of design. The great architect or designer—never a common commodity at best—may generate in a flash some brilliant concept and thus affect all future activity in the field. However, this individual, like the great scientist, has been laboriously storing data over years or decades in his private, built-in computer, and in the case of a building the idea can be developed only through thousands of hours of drudgery. In a first-class design organization, then, it appears that the creative component may not run to more than a fraction of a per cent of the total work required. Naturally, the percentage varies all over the lot. A dress designer, on the verge of changing the prevailing idea of proper styling through a bright new idea, has relatively little labor to realize his design compared to someone dealing with an involved structure or system. But in most design activity the percentage of time taken by truly creative work must be very small indeed.

This, then, takes us right to the computer, for this miracle tool has not yet pretended to creativity, and merely offers to reduce drudgery. If time-consuming, intellectually undemanding, and uninspired labor represents perhaps 85 per cent to 99.6 per cent of all work done in the design areas, then there is a loophole for the computer and its related instruments that looks larger to me than a barn door. In the last few years the new devices have begun to move in through the opening. The making of perspectives and other approximations of three-dimensional reality have always been skilled crafts. It takes a considerable amount of time to make such drawings. Now there are plotting machines that, if directed by a computer, can turn out such work quickly. There are also television-like screens that cannot only present such views directly, but rotate them as well, so that the object can be examined with ease from all angles. To match such performance using old methods would entail astronomical labor costs. Furthermore, with the cathode-tube presentations, the designer can use a "pencil" that not only modifies the visible drawing, but stores the new data in the computer. Architectural offices, along with engineers, are beginning to use computers to design structures, work that has traditionally employed armies of draftsmen. Lofting, an especially laborious form of drafting work needed for complex shapes such as boats and airplanes, is on the way out. Specification writing, also exceedingly cumbersome and time-consuming, is beginning to make use of the computer's capabilities. The same is true for the detailed statement of complex problems, such as hospitals, highways, and large office complexes. With considerable reductions in the cost of electronic devices now anticipated, it takes little imagination to forecast the future, as far as design organizations are concerned. The only thing that seems immune to the inroads of these machines is the creative act itself, and this, as we have seen, requires little in the way of time, space, or run-of-the-mill people.

A friend with whom I was discussing the subject matter of this paper, a sculptor of some renown, expressed the opinion that the computer might make rapid headway in many of the so-called "artistic" areas because the people working in them were, for the most part, not much good. He added hastily that such an opinion was not only subversive, but taboo, since it is an integral part of the American credo that "the people" must never be mentioned except as an agglomeration of individuals of inestimable value. From a religious or ethical point of view this may indeed be true, and certainly any politician who referred to "the people" in less than tones of abject adoration would hardly expect to be elected. What my friend was referring to was the rarely mentioned fact that in any area of activity, the great majority of individuals gainfully employed are incapable of making contributions of more than the most mediocre quality. I was jolted into awareness of this many years back, during a period when I ran a fair number of architectural competitions. I quickly learned that regardless of the number of entries—in several there were as many as two thousand—at least 90 per cent of the submissions were invariably of such abysmally poor quality that one wondered if their authors would be capable of holding a job pumping gas, let alone discharging their responsibilities as architects. If one should search for the reasons why America the Ugly is so ugly, here is one of them.

Our knowledge of people and their workings is still so primitive that it is impossible to say with any conviction why so high a percentage of the human race shows so low an order of capability. We have all heard about such factors as heredity, family background, prevailing social values, psychological conditioning, influences of the immediate environment, and education, but the explanation of almost any general question about people still eludes us. Pending the happy day when we understand more about ourselves, however, it may be taken as a fact the overwhelming majority of people everywhere has very little to contribute to the improvement of society or the race, or for that matter to itself. What I am getting at is the likelihood that the guaranteed income will go largely to people who might have very few ideas about what to do with it beyond indulging advertising-inculcated desires. Granted, with an income between one and two thousand dollars there is not much of a problem, for food bills alone would settle the question of what to do with the money. If it becomes possible to view the income as a true "plus," however, its disposition will reflect existing social values, which do not at the moment fill one with optimism. The main effect of this large flow of funds to consuming non-producers might be to stabilize to some extent the consumer goods industries.

In thinking of the design groups in this context, one wonders how many people in these essential professions are so imbued with enthusiasm for ideas of any kind that the new freedom given by a small guaranteed income might induce them to drop the hackwork they are doing and have a try at original research and study aimed at a creative contribution. One can become thoroughly pessimistic contemplating these possibilities, but there is another way of viewing the matter.

Let us assume that the consequences of doling out immense quantities of money to the aesthetically oriented groups and professions turns out to be enormously wasteful, in terms of general upgrading, or of getting positive social contributions from the recipients. For this possibility we have an ever-present example in nature. Many fish lay millions of eggs, very few of which survive. A pine forest produces cones with thousands of times as many seeds as can possibly attain maturity. The assumption here in connection with visible returns from the guaranteed income investment is that 99 per cent is "wasted"—that helps keep many people alive, but otherwise leaves them none the better for the assistance. The 99 per cent waste, however, leaves us with a 1 per cent "gain." Given a possible world population of five billion at the end of the millennium, 1 per cent equals fifty million people, or the combined populations of Scandanavia, Ireland, Switzerland, Holland, and Portugal. I am not prepared to debate any of these assumptions with an expert, but it is hard to escape the feeling that if fifty million people became more constructive, creative individuals, the gain in human resources would be rather spectacular. It is possible, of course, that the entire argument is pointless. We are reputed to pay, each year, some fifteen billion dollars for air pollution damage alone, and considerably more for saving this or that country from communism. Waste is the order of the day, and a little or lot more should not make much difference.

Of all the design fields we are considering here, the one most likely to be deeply affected by cybernation, possibly shattered, and in any case, transformed beyond recognition, is that of architecture. The argument I have been advancing is that artists, at the present moment, do not appear to be especially vulnerable, partly because of their aims and partly because of the flexibility of their methods of working. The designers do not have the artist's advantages, and furthermore, their methods of working, until yesterday, had changed relatively little over a long period of time. Since change is the order of the day, and since the working techniques of the architects in particular are especially cumbersome and old-fashioned, the vulnerability of this segment of the design professions seems to be close to maximum. But the problem goes deeper than questions like "who makes the drawings, men or machines?"

The role of the architect is much like that of the custom tailor. A tailor is a tradesman who makes a standard product (people do not vary greatly in size or configuration) as if it were a unique creation. We are all aware of what has happened to the custom tailor: statistically he just isn't, any more. The existence of the great couturier houses in Paris can be justified more easily, but even these establishments, despite fantastic publicity, only seem to be able to survive when they lend their names to mass-selling products such as stockings, perfume, and soap.

Like the tailor, the architect is asked by his clients to work out "personalized" solutions to standard problems—schools, churches, houses, multiple dwellings, office buildings, and the like. The threat to the architects is not only the computer, but the absolute necessity to standardize building components so that reasonable quality can be had at a reasonable cost. What this means is prefabrication of all sorts of building elements, a development that has been moving steadily forward. It also means complete industrial production of small units, such as dwellings and school classrooms, and this development has been advancing so rapidly that many housing markets are already dominated by the so-called "mobile homes." The architect now in practice is poorly equipped to deal with such situations, for his training has pointed him in the direction of the "gentleman designer" who dreams of turning out "individuality" for his mass-produced clients. Architects generally have little understanding of, or liking for the industrial process, nor do they yet understand that the destiny of most current building is to become something like three-dimensional Kleenex—great to use, but nothing to hand on to your grandchildren. Architects seem imbued with the notion that their job is to create monuments for posterity, while the society continues to languish because its most urgent needs are more rationally arranged cities, and not more fifty-story monuments to corporate egos.

A serious problem the architect faces along with those already mentioned is a problem of the custom tailors who still survive: fees. The tailor has to charge outrageous prices for suits that are only slightly better than the best mass-produced garments because he is trying to operate with handicrafts in a production-oriented society. The architect given a million-dollar project today will ask a fee of forty to eighty thousand dollars, which is a lot of money—but also completely insufficient to cope with the problems with which he is expected to deal. As a result, most buildings are hacked out and they look it. The glamorous new office buildings on New York's Park Avenue have for the most part been designed by "name" architects, and yet it is hard to find much to choose between one and another: despite all the efforts to make them look "different," the general effect is that of sameness, and if they were truly identical the avenue might be more attractive. Last week I saw just such a street under construction in Moscow and it looked very good indeed.

The architect, then, has some interesting problems. He is rapidly becoming in many ways an anachronism, but the fact that the building industry is a backward one gives him time to change. Many of the problems are beyond his control—archaic, chaotic building codes, for instance—and require a broader and more powerful type of social action than he can provide. The fact that his fees are expensive, but also inadequate for a good job, reflects the nation's habit of buying shelter on a handicraft basis. This is changing rapidly, however, simply because the unions have pushed the costs of their inefficient labor to a point where building becomes uneconomic. The architect's traditional view of building as a vehicle for his personal glorification leaves him ill-fitted for the inconspicuous role of a collaborator with industry, but there is evidence that the new generation coming out of the schools has a more realistic point of view.

There are immense opportunities for the architect in both large-scale planning and in merely satisfying part of the society's insatiable appetite for new construction. However, to cope adequately with present and coming problems a less antisocial attitude is needed, among other things. Perhaps the new generation will introduce the necessary changes. Nevertheless, there certainly appears to be a possibility of unemployment for draftsmen and other specialists whose work can be taken over by the computers, and one wonders what these people—hacks, mostly—will do with their free time even if guaranteed a roof, food, and some kind of transportation. Here again, as with the rest of the great mass of unneeded people, we have to place our bets and hopes on the hypothetical 1 per cent that might find constructive ways to use its new freedoms.

The third group, the craftsmen, is the most difficult to assess but also the most interesting in many ways. The crafts were destroyed as an economic force by technology, but the activity persists with astonishing vigor. Obviously the original basis for handicrafts—the need for manufactured products—no longer exists in a mass-production world, so other factors are in play.

The craftsman is characteristically identified with technically outmoded production methods for the simple reason that there are so few people who can afford modern factories for their personal enjoyment. If an individual can buy a potter's wheel, an electric kiln, a lathe or other simple power tools he is already doing rather well, for even these investments are not inconsiderable. One suspects, however, that if the personal economic limitations did not exist, these people would continue to work as they do for other reasons. The crafts play a new role in modern society precisely because of the ills from which the society suffers. As many writers have pointed out, a major change brought about by the Industrial Revolution was the fragmentation of work. The shoemaker who once designed his shoes, bought the materials, designed and manufactured the entire product was replaced by unskilled people who repetitively performed only parts of his work. The maker, in losing his earlier and healthier connection with work, presently became fragmented himself. The original creative act, even though modest, became mindless routine drudgery, the worker no longer had interest in what he was doing, and in many cases did not really understand *what* he was making. The process reached its insane and logical conclusion in the manufacture of the first nuclear bombs, when the workers were *forbidden* to know what they were making. Understandably, the decline in aesthetic standards was catastrophic, since there was no one to study the product as a whole, and words like "alienation" and "anomie," indicating an emotional crippling expressed as an inability to relate to society and other individuals, came into common use. The sick society of which we have all heard so much finds its origins in the beginnings of modern manufacturing, about two hundred years ago.

Given an environment in which the individual is anonymous and worthless except as a momentarily cheap production unit and emotionally disturbed to boot, the enormous appeal of craft activity is not hard to understand. The idea of creating *something all by oneself,* of rediscovering personal identity through work that permits total involvement, becomes irresistible. The individual who finds the world around him too unpleasant, too difficult to understand or cope with, has a marvelous escape through the crafts. He may participate as a part-time worker or hobbyist, but if he develops better than average capability, there is also the possibility that he can flee the polluted city with his family, depart from the two-dimensional pseudo-world of organization men, and set up as a self-supporting economic unit. Many have done this. They represent, of course, the intelligent, capable, energetic minority, but in societies as large as our own minorities can become fairly sizable.

The use of crafts as an economically viable way of life is becoming more and more possible, for the same reasons people turned to them in the first place. As industry-produced items proliferate, the contents of stores the world over take on a certain look of sameness. The work of the individual craftsman, in this context, takes on new value in the eyes of the shopper because it is identifiable as something special, even unique. In other words, in an affluent environment conspicuously lacking in genuine satisfactions and pleasures, the crafts now have an extraordinarily appealing message to both consumers and makers.

The search for some activity, however humble, that helps the individual identify himself as a somebody rather than a statistic embraces the hobbies as well as the crafts. Have you ever watched a model railroad club in action on a Saturday? The intensity of involvement is really quite remarkable, and one cannot but wonder what would happen if paid work elicited the same kind of interest. There are millions who find relief from the deadliness of existence in making models of trains, cars, boats, and planes. Thousands more are devoted to automotive hobbies that can be carried to some pretty spectacular conclusions in terms of custom cars. The difference between the hobbyist (leaving out enthusiasts like stamp collectors, who do not *make* things) and the craftsman cannot be found in any sharp dividing line. By my own definition, both may display a high degree of skill, but the craftsman often *designs* what he makes, whereas the hobbyist almost invariably *reproduces* something. The crafts, therefore, always contain the possibility of approaching the emotional and intellectual level typical of the arts at their best.

The implications of all this are considerable, from a social point of view. The craftsman, like the artist, tends to be immune to the direct effects of cybernation. He may be fully aware of microelectronics, lasers, tape-actuated production lines, and all the rest of our technological baggage, but he has no need for it in his work, nor is there any way technological development can obsolete him. He is thus saved from the scrap pile of people, which will presently be as large as the piles of wrecked cars. We have noted the very real possibility that the demand for his wares—if he makes them for sale—will increase. The prospect, therefore, is a renaissance of outmoded technology to be used for human rather than commercial purposes.

For all the people in this area, the guaranteed income might have great significance in terms of life itself, for it could open the door to meaningful productive activity, pursued not as a livelihood but as a means of personal fulfillment. The existence of economic security might help millions to find the courage to turn their backs on an existence that too often has all the charm of a rat race. In suggesting this possibility, I see no contradiction with earlier uncomplimentary remarks about the mediocre qualities exhibited by the majority of individuals. *We simply do not know* what people might be capable of under different conditions of life and work. The guaranteed income, viewed in this sense, becomes a sociological tool for revealing to us more about ourselves than we know right now.

It would be entertaining indeed if one of the massive results of the triumph of technology were the return of the amateur. The word itself, which has its roots in the Latin verb "to love," suggests something that has largely disappeared from the scene: the participant who loves what he is doing. It was the amateur who sparked some of the greatest creative moments in our history—the eighteenth century, the Italian Renaissance, Periclean Greece. We could use him. He might turn out to be the most effective antidote to our spreading sickness, the only alternative to LSD, kicks, and freaking out, the main carrier of a fresh meaning of life which somehow got mislaid in our glorious, unthinking climb from rags to riches.

TAX IMPLICATIONS

Kendall P. Cochran

INTRODUCTION

We assume, as a point of departure, that the basic forces described by Irving Kaplan will continue, and that as a consequence, employment opportunities will decrease in the market-directed sector of the economy, while productivity continues to increase, and at an accelerated rate. His reading of past industrial and scientific trends may, of course, be inaccurate. If so, his reading of the future is probably incorrect. If his forecast is wrong, if scientific development ceases, or if it escalates into a nuclear holocaust, then clearly any concern with the implications of a guaranteed annual income are irrelevant.

In our opinion, however, the essential details of his forecast are correct. And if this does prove to be the case, then some form of a guaranteed annual income will be an indispensable part of the productive-distributive mechanism of tomorrow's economy.

A basic premise of this essay is that the economic system can no longer measure individual productive "contribution." We conclude, however, that each *being* is entitled to a share of the currently produced goods and services. We would hold this to be true, not only for dogs and whooping cranes, but also for humans. Above this base, additional shares of the total output should be distributed for special services to society: to Lassie for making motion pictures, to college professors for teaching (or something), to Guy Lombardo for reviving old songs.

As we move into an economy of increasing productivity,

and decreasing employment opportunities, we see no real alternative to some form of a guaranteed annual income. The implementation of a guaranteed annual income will obviously necessitate drastic changes in our social and moral and political fabric—changes that will be extremely difficult to accept, since they will be in direct conflict with those habits of thought currently held to be eternally true. But this will not be the first time society has been called upon to reassess its basic institutions and to realign them to conform to emerging industrial and scientific trends.

As a matter of fact, economics, as a separate academic discipline, began under precisely those auspices in 1776, when Adam Smith's *Wealth of Nations* launched economics as a new branch of moral philosophy. This remarkable book also ushered in a new era in political philosophy, providing as it did the philosophical rationalization for laissez-faire.

Smith did not really invent anything particularly new. What he did, and did extremely well, was to codify then-emerging economic values and practices into a logical and coherent philosophical system. In Wesley Mitchell's words, he provided a "neat philosopher's rationalization for what the bourgeois were doing, or wanting to do." And what the bourgeois wanted was more freedom from government regulation. Smith deftly provided the answer in the interplay of several economic forces: the profit motive, a free labor market, the rights of private property, and the invisible hand of free competition.

As the industrial economy grew and expanded in the nineteenth century, the economic rewards were practically unlimited for the few who found their way to the top, but too many remained at the bottom, cold, hungry, and downtrodden. True, there was no real alternative, for the eternal fact of economic life was poverty. The spector of unrelenting, grinding scarcity lay always on the land. Consequently, exploitation, injustice, and degradation were the simple and inescapable facts of economic life.

Now, however, scarcity and low productivity are no longer our pressing economic problems. As a consequence, there is no longer any economic reason for poverty. The pressing problem now is to find methods to distribute our productive potential. That is, we produce a prodigious quantity of houses, automobiles, food, clothing, recreation, schools, factories, etc., which are then distributed to those who have a money income. Any money income, however derived, entitles one to partake of current production according to the amount of income at hand. It is at exactly this point—the distributive mechanism—where the economy is potentially in serious trouble. And it is at this point—the distributive mechanism—that some form of guaranteed annual income becomes economically necessary. Our antiquated distributive mechanism is inefficient and inadequate to the needs of today; it will soon be a serious liability as this newest revolution, that of automation and cybernation, continues.

The specific problem to be solved at this time is how to distribute the output of goods and services that can be produced now and in the future.

For roughly two hundred years we have tried to equate the right to partake *of* production with one's contribution *to* production. In other words, we have relied on the so-called impersonal forces of the market to reward each factor of production according to his individual productive effort.

This was not too difficult so long as we remained a nation of small farmers and innkeepers. Many forces, however, have long since destroyed that simple world. The trust and holding company on the one hand, the assembly line and the machine process on the other, have homogenized this productive process. It is thus impossible for the market to measure the productive contribution of an individual worker on the assembly line. It is equally impossible for the market to determine how many dividends a stockholder has "earned" when the company has issued no new stock in half a century.

In sum, we have long ago abandoned any pretext of rewarding each member of society according to his productive contribution since there simply is no way of measuring it in this highly interdependent, homogenized industrial complex.

Instead, we reward each participant, and each non-participant, according to relative positions of power and prestige. This is why deans are paid more than professors, whites more than Negroes, and men more than women. It has nothing to do with productive contribution, only with power and prestige. This is the fundamental issue with which the guaranteed income is concerned: to abolish power and prestige as the sole criteria by which the productive capacity of the economy is distributed. Our ability to produce goods and services staggers comprehension, and that ability will undoubtedly continue to expand in the future. Since we cannot produce unless we find ways of consuming it, some form of a guaranteed annual income is necessary. We cannot long continue to link industrial productivity to a system of distribution based upon power and prestige. We cannot long continue to enjoy both plenty and privilege.

THE EVOLUTION OF TAX POLICY

The acceptance of society's economic commitment to all members of society will require a shift in many governmental rules and responsibilities. An obvious beginning will be the abandonment of all direct welfare measures such as social security, old age assistance, farm price supports, etc., while expanding such indirect measures for distributing the nation's productive capacity as greater aid to education, free medical care for the young as well as the old, adequate housing for all, etc. Currently accepted philosophies and practices of taxation will also be revised.

The basic goal of tax policy in the future will be to ensure that the potential productive output of the economy will be in fact realized because there are adequate incomes available to all. This will be the third major chapter in the evolution of taxes since the emergence of the market economy.

Adam Smith wrote an admirable explanation and defense of the first chapter. The duties of the sovereign were to be limited to three essential functions: national defense, justice, and certain public works. Taxes were also to be limited to support of those functions that should be provided for by "the general contribution of the whole society." Individuals could go to the market and buy meat and potatoes, but not courts of law, national defense, or lighthouses. And, as might be expected, this basic view of taxation is accepted by many today. Another Smith, writing in 1961, echoed that 1776 philosophy when he asserted: "Taxes are compulsory payments which individual citizens make, directly and indirectly, for services provided by the government . . . Private incomes are [thus] diverted from private consumption to joint or public consumption."[1]

We cannot quarrel with the Smith Brothers since this is *one* function of tax policy. Quite obviously if the resources of the community are fully employed, then an increase in taxes will divert production from one sector to another. This, however, is much too limited a view of tax policy.

The second chapter in the evolution of tax philosophy must be credited to another economist, John Maynard Keynes. His *General Theory* published in 1936 was truly a revolutionary work in economic theory and marked the beginning of a far-ranging social-political revolution.

Briefly stated, Keynes explained why the economy can at times operate at less than full employment. His explanation was soon adopted by most economists. Not so by the general public, however, for acceptance of this theory called for drastic revisions in traditional concepts of government finance. One of the most sanctified of fiscal guidelines, the annually

[1] Dan Throop Smith, *Federal Tax Reform* (New York: McGraw-Hill, 1961), pp. 2–3.

balanced budget, was summarily discarded. Contemporary "countercyclical" fiscal policy uses federal taxing and spending as levers to alter the level of aggregate demand and thus to influence quite directly the level of employment and prices and the rate of economic growth. Tax rates and the tax revenues generated are examined by the yardstick of full employment, stable prices, and the rate of economic growth—and not merely as a means of diverting private incomes to public consumption. While it is true that large segments of the public (particularly newspaper editors) have not been persuaded of this philosophy, the revolution is nevertheless fairly complete. The tax cut of 1964, for example, was specifically designed to stimulate a laggard economy. The results were so dramatic that many lingering doubters were won over, including both presidential candidates in the 1964 election.

While there is no doubt that the total level of economic activity can be significantly altered by appropriate fiscal policy, there are serious limitations. The most serious is inherent in the very reason for its success: countercyclical fiscal policy is powerfully effective because its impact is directly on effective demand. An increase in the demand for goods and services will stimulate higher levels of employment, and therefore higher incomes for those employed. But the necessary link is *employment*. To be effective, people have to be employed— or employable. And so long as the vast majority of the labor force is either employed or employable, then countercyclical fiscal policy will be a valuable and powerful tool with which to pursue worthy social goals.

If, however, the future of the industrial economy is to be found in the spread of automation, then countercyclical tax and spending policies will inevitably have less and less impact on the total economy. This is why some form of guaranteed annual income is inevitable. It is also why a change is inevitable in the philosophy and practice of taxation. In short, we are on the threshold of a third chapter in the evolution of taxation philosophy, where the basic goal will be to ensure the success of the guaranteed annual income. The general outlines of such a tax program can already be discerned—in part, if not fully.

THE NEGATIVE INCOME TAX

Several economists have, in recent years, proposed some form of a negative income tax.[2] The basic idea is quite simple: since the administrative machinery is already in effect, and is highly automated, the income tax mechanism would be used as a simple and expeditious means of distributing income payments to the poor. Everybody would be required to file an income tax report, and those in the lower brackets would receive a "rebate" which would partially close the gap between actual earnings and some level of income that has been defined as being the minimum necessary. To realize this minimum income, each person would have to contribute some private earnings.

Partially closing the gap, however, will never eliminate poverty, since it could not provide the necessary income for the unemployables. Reducing the poverty gap may dull the fangs of poverty, but it obviously can never eliminate them. Nor can any such halfway measure meet the real need for some kind of a guaranteed annual income. The real need for such a plan stems, not merely from the needs of the poor for a higher standard of living, but from the prodigious productive ability of the modern industrial economy, and the increasingly impossible task of measuring the productive contribution of any individual.

This is exactly what Theobald has urged with his two-part proposal for a guaranteed annual income. The first part is the

[2] *See*, e.g. Milton Friedman, *Capitalism and Freedom* (University of Chicago Press, 1965), pp. 190–95; Robert J. Lampman, *American Economic Review*, 55:2 (May 1965), 521–29; James Tobin, *Dædalus*, 94 (1965), pp. 891–905.

Basic Economic Security (BES) program. This would guarantee some minimum, say $1,250 for an adult and $750 for a child. If actual earnings are below this, then a direct payment would bring total income at least up to this minimum, and above it for those with other earnings.

The second and distinctive part of Theobald's proposed guaranteed annual income is the Committed Spending (CS) proposal. This is designed "to protect the existing middle income group against abrupt major declines in their standard of living." When those in the middle income groups lose jobs due to automation, or other abrupt shifts of economic power, they would be entitled to the CS payments, based on previous earnings.

The details of both a BES and a CS program remain to be evolved in the light of experience and growing abundance. Both will clearly be needed, however. The economic problem of the future will not be merely raising the level of subsistence of the very poor. That we can do fairly easily. The really difficult problem will be to find devices (rationalizations) that will permit us to distribute an enormously productive flow of goods and services with little or no direct reference to productive contribution as measured in the market. If this is to be realized, a thorough revision of our tax structure will be mandatory.

AN APPROPRIATE TAX STRUCTURE

Our task in this context is not to set forth the details of some future federal tax structure. Computers, aided perhaps by economists and statisticians armed with necessary data, will do it with great precision. Given what we believe will be the aim of that tax structure—to ensure the success of a guaranteed annual income and the full utilization of our productive capacity, we can, however, describe the general outlines of a tax structure appropriate to that aim. This description will necessarily be brief and will assume some familiarity with current tax practices.[3]

THE PERSONAL INCOME TAX

In brief, an appropriate personal income tax will be based on a progressive tax rate beginning at some point above the guaranteed annual income, applicable to all income received, with few deductions permitted. Since this represents a rather drastic departure from current and traditional practices, the basic details will be examined.

TAXABLE INCOME

All income, from whatever source derived, must be subject to a progressive tax structure at the federal level. Thus, current practices which give favored tax treatment to certain kinds of income, would all be eliminated.

Two of the more pressing needs are the abolition of favored tax treatment of capital gains and interest on municipal securities: both should be treated as any other form of income for tax purposes.

Gains from the sale or exchange of a financial asset are currently treated most favorably with the maximum tax rate applicable to such financial gains being 25 per cent, compared to a maximum tax rate of 70 per cent on ordinary income. This single favorable treatment, more than all other factors combined, explains the actual regressivity of the current federal income tax structure at upper levels. The effective tax

[3] For a comprehensive and detailed analysis of current tax policies, *see* Joseph A. Pechman, *Federal Tax Policy*, Washington, D.C.: The Brookings Institution, 1966; Richard B. Goode, *The Individual Income Tax*, Washington, D.C.: The Brookings Institution, 1964; and Harold M. Groves, *Financing Government*, New York: Holt, 1964.

rate increases, if somewhat moderately, as incomes increase, up to about $150,000. But at about that point, because of the capital gains tax, the effective rate actually paid decreases.[4]

Capital gains need not be treated *exactly* as if they were ordinary income, such as wages or salaries regularly received. Capital losses could be deducted from gains before taxes are computed, and large, intermittent gains could be averaged out over several years for tax purposes. But technical adjustments aside, there will be no defensible reason for continuing this favored treatment.

It is commonly alleged that this lower tax rate is necessary to encourage risk-taking in business enterprise because the high rates applicable to ordinary income discourage venture capital from finding its way into new and untried paths. This argument may have been plausibly true in the day of rugged individualism and the solitary Yankee inventor. But it is not a very persuasive argument in the industrialized, automated world of today where real investment in plant and equipment is dominated by the large, well-to-do, already established corporation. It alone can finance and undertake new and risky capital expenditures. Although folklore tenaciously holds to the contrary, current empirical research has shattered the belief that high tax rates discourage productive effort.[5]

The most significant impact of this tax on individuals is to encourage *speculative* financial ventures in corporate stocks and real estate.[6] "Buy cheap, hold, and sell dear" is indeed risk-taking from an individual point of view. But when the risk is only in terms of buying and selling outstanding assets (such as corporate stocks or land), then society itself has taken no risk in the use of its economic resources. There is, therefore, no reason to treat this individual speculative risk any differently then we do the two-dollar bettor at the race-

[4] Goode, p. 236.

[5] *See,* e.g. Robin Barlow, Harvey E. Brazer, and James N. Morgan, *Economic Behavior of the Affluent,* Washington, D.C.: The Brookings Institution, 1966, esp. chap. x.

[6] *Ibid.,* chap. IX.

track. He too is taking a risk when he "invests" his venture capital. Speedy Tom, his favorite in the Third at Hialeah, may in fact turn and run the other way—in which case he has lost his capital. The fact remains, he is not risking the community's economic resources and neither is the stock speculator. Neither should be given favored tax treatment—unless, of course, we wish to subsidize betting, on stocks or on horses. If this be a desirable social goal, then we should do it directly and not corrupt our tax structure with lower taxes for such financial gains.

The same point applies equally to the taxation of interest received from municipal and state securities. Since this is a tax-free income, the agency issuing them pays a significantly lower rate of interest than would otherwise be required. This gives local and state governments a competitive edge in capital markets, since without this tax subsidy, they would have to compete with established corporate bonds. Many smaller towns and villages might have to pay a higher rate of interest than a nationally known corporation. So goes the defense of the status quo.

This argument is probably true, for without the tax-free status, a small village in South Carolina would probably have to pay a higher rate of interest on its bonds than AT&T does. Since this income is tax-exempt, savings in upper income groups are obviously attracted to these securities, and they are used to finance various long-term local improvements, ranging from new streets and schools to locally owned public utilities and industrial development tracts designed to attract new business. There is no doubt that many of these local activities do need subsidizing since the need for local schools, streets, waterworks, etc., is not directly related to local tax rolls. This demands only that the subsidy be open and direct, however, and not built into the income tax structure where the result is a distortion in the intended rate structure, a resulting loss of tax revenues, and a tax-free income to a favored few.

This unequal treatment of taxpayers is in no way justifiable, since there is no defensible reason why income earned on savings should be tax free for some and not for others. This shelter should be eliminated in future issues of state and municipal securities.

INCOME SPLITTING

Although in most families, the total income is earned by one person, community property laws in several states permitted a husband and wife to divide the family income in half, and then pay the lower tax rate applicable to each half. This was a tremendous tax advantage for married couples living in these states, particularly for those with higher incomes, so in 1948, Congress extended this provision to all married couples by permitting them to file a "Joint Return." The major impact of income splitting is to levy higher tax rates on single taxpayers. The single taxpayer may have both children and dependent parents, but irrespective of family obligations, to qualify for the lower effective tax rates, there must be a spouse. (Under certain conditions a taxpayer with dependents, but no spouse, may qualify for the tax status of "head of household." This is a rate structure somewhat higher than that applicable to single persons and somewhat lower than that for married couples.)

There seems no sound reason for this discriminatory treatment of non-married taxpayers. There are two possible rationalizations, however: marriage should be encouraged, and/or married families have higher living expenses. Differences in living expenses should be accounted for by the exemption allowance, which accords equal treatment to everyone, married spouse or not. If we wish to encourage marriage by some form of subsidy, and there is no sound economic reason why we should not, then it should be done by direct subsidy—

say a bonus, payable perhaps one month after the wedding. Better that, than to distort the tax structure of federal income taxes.

DEDUCTIONS

In sum, all income, from whatever source derived, must be included if we are to have an equitable tax base. Veteran's benefits, capital gains, corporate dividends, and interest on municipal securities should be taxed at the same rate as wages and salaries. The same tax rate should apply to the same income, irrespective of the marital status of the taxpayer. And the overall tax structure must necessarily be a progressive one —where the marginal tax rate increases as taxable income increases. This is precisely what current federal tax rates do, ranging from a minimum of 14 per cent to a maximum of 70 per cent. But these rates are an outrageous illusion, since the maximum rate actually paid is only 33 per cent (on the average) for incomes of about $150,000.

Income splitting, tax-free incomes, and the maximum of 25 per cent on capital gains account for most of this discrepancy between nominal and actual rates. There are, however, still other serious inequities built into our practice of allowing deductions in computing taxable income. These deductions represent no consistent philosophy of taxation; they are merely the accumulation of decades of tampering with the tax structure to achieve a variety of social or political or moral goals.

Certain limited deductions, and exemptions must be subtracted from total income to arrive at an equitable income figure for tax purposes. But if the final tax structure is to implement its intended goal of a workable guaranteed annual income, then major revisions in current practices regarding deductions will be mandatory.

A good maxim back on the farm was "to pick the goose

with a minimum of squawking." Apparently most legislators have translated this maxim to the income tax code, for the potential taxpayer who made the most noise has been plucked the least. Barnyard philosophy may have been adequate in the barnyard, but it will prove to be the Achilles' heel of a meaningful tax structure for tomorrow's economy. Since most current deductions must be eliminated, and since this represents another rather radical departure from current practices, a brief explanation is in order.

STATE AND LOCAL TAXES

Approximately 50 per cent of all state and local tax payments qualify as legitimate business expenses and are, therefore, deductible for federal tax purposes.[7] Since these are necessary costs incurred in earning an income, and since the income itself is subject to the federal income tax, such tax payments should be continued as deductions.

An equitable tax structure, however, would eliminate state and local tax payments as personal deductions. The effects of such deductions on the federal tax structure are obvious. By reducing the tax base, higher nominal tax rates are required, and the progressivity of the tax structure is therefore lessened. To illustrate: if A and B each pay $100 in local taxes, and if A is subject to a 14 per cent tax rate, then his federal tax liability is reduced by $14. If B is subject to the 70 per cent rate, then his federal tax liability is reduced by $70. The effect, then, is for the U. S. Treasury to return a $14 subsidy to taxpayer A and a $70 subsidy to taxpayer B, thus reinforcing the regressivity of the local tax structure and contributing further to its basic inequities.

But effects aside, there is neither an economic nor a constitutional justification for allowing taxes to be deducted. The "indirect subsidy" justification should be briefly noted:

[7] Goode, p. 176.

Citizens will presumably offer less resistance to a local tax increase if such taxes are deductible. State and local governments may, therefore, be less constrained about imposing or increasing taxes, and thus more willing to assume fiscal responsibility for local problems. Or so the argument goes.[8]

There is, of course, no way of knowing if this is true. But true or not, it does not justify the continuance of present practices. If local governments encounter citizen resistance to higher tax rates, or if they fear intimidating business, the answer must be a greater reliance on a comprehensive federal tax program and federal grants-in-aid. This approach has significantly increased in importance in recent years, and will undoubtedly continue into the future.

MEDICAL EXPENSES

The only justification for allowing medical expenses as a deduction is to provide some measure of tax relief since catastrophic medical expense obviously eliminates current income as a measure of ability to pay taxes.

We assume, however, that as society moves toward the acceptance of a guaranteed annual income, it will also adopt a broad-based and comprehensive medical insurance program. Since medical expenses will then no longer be paid out of current income, there will no longer be any justification for allowing them to be deducted.

INTEREST PAID

When an individual has borrowed money as a necessary adjunct to acquiring an income, any interest paid on that loan should of course be deductible since the income earned will be taxable.

[8] This argument was summarized by Goode, pp. 177–78.

This reasoning does not extend, however, to personal consumer debt incurred to finance a washing machine, a vacation, or even a new home. It is often urged (particularly by savings and loan banks) that this deduction encourages home ownership, and since it is obviously good for families to own their own homes, this deduction should be continued. This is not the place to debate the merits of home ownership, nor indeed whether this practice even encourages it. In any event, if we deem it advisable to subsidize housing, then we should do it directly—and not by tampering with the income tax.

A guaranteed annual income would be an ideal technique to achieve this goal, allowing, as it would, some minimum amount to be spent on housing, according to the wishes of the recipient. We could also provide public housing, or we could give a direct subsidy to those who wished to bask in the warmth of their own cottage. There are, in short, many ways to encourage home ownership, and nearly all of them, we suggest, would be more effective than allowing interest payments on a home mortgage to be a deductible item.

The elimination of this deduction would also eliminate one of the more flagrant tax dodges available to a select few: the purchasing of large "cash-value" insurance policies with loans from the same insurance company. Since the interest on the loan is currently deductible, the net cost is negligible for those subject to higher tax rates.[9]

CASUALTY LOSSES

While the practice has varied in the past, current tax law allows all casualty losses in excess of $100 as a deductible item, presumably to allow some measure of relief. This presumption, however, is erroneous, since a $100 floor is unrelated either to hardship, or to the ability to pay taxes in any

---

[9] This tax dodge is explained in greater detail by Smith, pp. 100–1.

given year. The only significant beneficiary of this provision is the taxpayer in the high income bracket, who can, in effect, insure himself (at a saving of seventy cents on the dollar) against such losses. But since that taxpayer can protect himself against such losses with ordinary insurance, there is in fact no justification to subsidize him through income tax deductions.

GIFTS TO CHARITY

If a patron of the arts chances on a good bargain and buys a painting for say, $10,000, and later gives it to a museum—after it has been reappraised for $100,000—his charitable inclinations will be more than amply rewarded. If he is in the 50 per cent tax bracket, his tax liability will be reduced by $50,000. This, a five-fold return on his investment, is almost as rewarding as the capital gains game.

The IRS recently scrutinized some four hundred donated works of art that were originally purchased for $1,471,562; by income tax time, the "fair market value" had increased to $5,811,905. In only three of the four hundred cases scrutinized had the "fair market value" actually declined between time of purchase and contribution to charity.[10] With the friendly cooperation of interested museums and appraisers, this kind of gift-giving has become an easy tactic to reduce the tax liability for those in the upper income brackets. It must obviously be eliminated.

There remains, however, the broader question of whether charitable contributions should be deductible. There is little direct evidence that deductibility in fact encourages charitable contributions, except in the upper tax brackets. Personal support of the church, the Red Cross, the March of Dimes, etc., is, we suspect, largely a matter of personal whim or conviction, and thus little influenced by tax considerations. The

[10] *Wall Street Journal*, January 3, 1967.

same probably cannot be said, however, for large-scale support of a museum, art gallery, or research institution. The question simply is whether, by making large cash contributions tax deductible, we want the government, through tax revenue lost, to be a joint underwriter of such organizations.

A $50,000 gift at the 50 per cent tax bracket costs the giver $25,000 and the Treasury the other $25,000 in lost revenues. Again, this is lost revenue that will have to be raised elsewhere. But because of our long tradition, and because of the widely diversified agencies currently dependent on private contributions, it would probably be advisable to maintain cash contributions as deductions—at least in some limited form. A workable solution might be to allow a cash contribution, but only when it exceeds perhaps 4 per cent, and not in excess of 20 per cent of income. An upper ceiling would be advisable in order to limit the Treasury's contribution in each tax year. If the taxpayer wishes to underwrite a favorite charity to an extent exceeding this ceiling, he could of course do so, but at his own expense. Old works of art would, however, be eliminated as deductible items, making the whole tax system more equitable. And as a by-product, it would reduce possible collusion between donor, recipient, and appraiser. Any small step to discourage dishonesty will, of course, be welcomed by all except the conspirators.

EXEMPTIONS

Beginning with the first income tax law of 1913, we have exempted a certain amount of income from taxes according to the number of dependents. The basic idea is of course one of equity—an attempt to equalize after-tax income per family member. A couple with an income of $5,000 presumably has a higher per capita income (and ability to pay taxes) than a family with the same income and eight children. The *personal exemption* is a simple and straightforward attempt to redress this kind of inequality. The income tax we are outlining would, for the same reasons, include a personal exemption, but not one for blindness or old age. Their special income needs should be met by other devices.

We cannot establish what the future personal exemption should be since this will depend on the future GNP, population, rate of economic growth, and the amount of the guaranteed annual income. It would seem sensible, initially, to exempt an amount equal to the guaranteed income.

THE PERSONAL INCOME TAX: A SUMMARY

If an equitable guaranteed annual income is to be a meaningful component of an expanding industrial economy, then our concepts regarding the philosophy and practice of tax policy will have to be revised and replaced.

But rather than serve merely as a vehicle to transfer private incomes to finance public works, and by manipulation to achieve a variety of social goals through indirect subsidies, the philosophy and practice of taxation must become an integral part of the income distributive mechanism of the economy. Since its distinctive function will be to complement the guaranteed annual income, its major characteristic will be its simplicity—each receiving unit would:

1. Add up all income from every source.
2. Deduct:
    A. Specified expenses incurred acquiring that income
    B. Gifts to charity within specified limits
    C. Personal exemptions
3. Equals: taxable income

The taxpayer would then consult the current tax table to determine taxes due for the year. These could be either negative or positive, depending on the type of distributive mechanism adopted. The precise rates cannot, of course, be calculated for the future. But as an indication, had we used a similar income tax structure in 1963, a positive tax rate ranging from 10 per cent to 40 per cent would have yielded approximately the same total revenue as did the 20 per cent to 91 per cent rate structure applicable that year.

THE CORPORATION INCOME TAX

The tax on corporate income will remain an integral part of the overall federal tax structure for several reasons: it provides some countercyclical stability and generates a tremendous amount of revenue (second only to the personal income tax). It also ensures that the personal income tax will remain as equitable as intended, for if corporations were not taxed, individuals would find it to their tax advantage to incorporate. Furthermore, with the growth of the large, impersonal corporation, the distinction between ownership and management has become increasingly blurred[11]—and as a result, it creates income to which nobody has a legitimate personal claim. Its net earnings are truly *corporate* income, quite separate and distinct from its owners, managers, or employees, and therefore subject to a separate tax.

The difficult task is to determine this taxable net income. In the abstract, it would seem a simple task: gross earnings minus expenses incurred in acquiring those earnings. But as is true of the individual income tax, the definition of what is "deductible" has been repeatedly changed in an attempt to achieve a variety of goals. The most notable examples are the depreciation and depletion schedules. If a manufacturing concern buys a box of paper clips, this is clearly a legitimate business expense. The same is true of interest on borrowed money, wages paid to employees, and salaries paid to execu-

[11] *See*, e.g. Adolf A. Berle, Jr., *Power Without Property*, New York: Harcourt, 1959.

tives. But when a machine, lasting several years, must be purchased, the entire cost of the machine is clearly not a business expense in the current year. So quite correctly, the manufacturer is allowed to depreciate this over several years.

And this is where the difficulty originates. Traditionally the company figured the expected life of the machine and allocated the cost in equal amounts over that many years. In an attempt to stimulate new capital spending, Congress has revised traditional procedures and allowed businesses a choice of methods for computing depreciation. Further attempts to stimulate new capital spending occurred in 1962 when businesses were allowed to deduct 7 per cent of their new capital spending from their corporate profits tax liability. Flexible and realistic depreciation schedules pose no insurmountable problem, however. The Treasury could calculate reasonable alternatives that realistically reflect actual depreciation, which is of course a necessary cost of production.

Serious inequities remain, however, in the extractive industries (oil, gas, etc.). These industries have been granted a "depletion allowance," in lieu of depreciation. These depletion allowances, at first limited to oil and natural gas, have been extended to nearly all extractive industries and are an extremely lucrative subsidy. Since this allowance (27 per cent on petroleum) is a tax-free income to the owner of the industry (individual or corporation), it seriously distorts the overall tax structure, both individual and corporate. Recent reports of the U. S. Treasury, for example, cite the cases of several individuals with annual incomes as high as 26 million dollars, who paid not one penny in income tax. The average tax paid by all U.S. corporations averages some 49 per cent; for the major oil companies, it is as low as 12 per cent.[12]

Depletion allowances must be eliminated. Necessary costs of exploration, drilling, and extracting should continue to be

[12] Philip M. Stern, *The Great Treasury Raid* (New York: The New American Library), p. 35.

deductible (though not as generously as they are now), but the additional subsidy of the tax-free income vis-à-vis the depletion allowance must be eliminated.

Another important change will be to permit corporations to treat dividends paid to stockholders exactly as they do interest paid to bondholders: as a necessary cost of doing business and hence deductible before taxes are paid. Since for tax purposes, the corporation should be recognized as a separate productive unit, all necessary expenses (including dividends) must be deducted to arrive at a correct tax base. As a productive unit, the corporation pays the manager his salary, the bondholder his interest, the workingman his wage. By the same "right," the stockholder is entitled to his dividend. In each case this becomes income to the individual and subject to the applicable individual income tax rate. There is no reason why the current two-step progressive rate could not be extended to several steps, perhaps a range of from 10 to 50 per cent. The precise range of rates would have to be calculated in light of the revised net income arrived at by the alternate method suggested above.

EXCISE TAXES

Although we've only had one whiskey rebellion, excise taxes have never been very popular. Their only justification is that they do raise money rather easily. However, as a tax on spending, they are regressive; they do redistribute real income *from* lower income groups proportionately more than from those at higher levels. Extensive use of such taxes would seriously impede the social goals sought with a guaranteed annual income. They should therefore be abolished.

Fortunately, Congress has already taken a major step in this direction and by 1969 most federal excise taxes will have been repealed. The only significant ones then remaining will be the sumptuary taxes on liquor and tobacco, user taxes on gasoline, and regulatory taxes on gambling, narcotics, etc. At a minimum, these will probably remain in force for a long time, irrespective of a guaranteed annual income, or the arguments of an economist. Excessively high taxes will be levied on liquor and tobacco so long as there is a prevailing (even minority) belief that their consumption should be minimized, if not eliminated. Gasoline taxes will remain so long as social forces dictate the use of the automobile as an individualized means of transportation. And so long as we do want to regulate certain activities without outlawing them, then minor taxes on such activities (gambling for example) will be enacted. Arguments involving equity and/or the allocation of resources are totally unrelated to these taxes.

PAYROLL TAXES

The social security (OASDHI) "contribution" and the unemployment compensation tax would be among the very first taxes to be abolished—if an effective guaranteed annual income is adopted.

The OASDHI tax (currently 4.4 per cent by both employee and employer on the first $6,600 of income) was designed to finance retirement and disability benefits, and more recently health insurance benefits, to those who have worked a minimum number of months in "covered" employment. Since it is a flat rate, with a $6,600 maximum tax base, it is obviously a very regressive tax, shifting purchasing power from the lower and middle income recipients to the retired or disabled beneficiaries.[13]

It is also relatively clear that many employers pass their share of the tax on to consumers in the form of higher prices.

[13] Margaret S. Gordon, *The Economics of Welfare Policies* (Columbia University Press, 1963), pp. 24, 43–44.

This is particularly true of the larger, more powerful employer who has a strategic position of power in the market. Those who are not so powerful, the self-employed, small firms and small farms, corner groceries, employers of domestics, etc., probably absorb this tax, which only contributes to its regressivity—and the inevitable consequence is that their employees are likewise exempt from these benefits. It is indeed a curious method of providing economic security.

A contributory tax was purposefully selected to finance the social security program, in the belief that those who benefit from the program should directly finance it. This analogy is in error, however, when applied to a tax designed to provide retirement benefits, since any tax is simply a means of transferring *current* purchasing from the taxpayer to the beneficiary. Tax funds cannot be accumulated until time for retirement. But most important, when society decides to provide a basic income to all, then all arguments for a contributory tax become moot and simply irrelevant.

Eventually, the same reasoning will lead to the abolishment of the unemployment compensation tax and the benefits supported by that tax. One of the major goals of this program, according to Professor L. A. Lester, was "The assurance of compensation as a matter of right to those regularly attached to the labor market."[14] But two out of five gainfully employed are not even covered. These include those least able to protect themselves: agricultural workers, domestic employees, employees with small firms, etc. Even for those who are covered, the actual benefit payment during unemployment is very low. It was this very inadequacy that has prompted the stronger unions to secure company-financed supplementary unemployment benefits (SUB). Some 2.3 million workers are now covered by SUB and some plans are really quite liberal, granting total benefits as high as 85 per cent of regular pay, and guaranteeing SUB payments for as long as

[14] Quoted in *ibid.*, p. 78.

five years. Some plans even use these funds, when they are not needed to cover unemployment, to finance vacation and retirement allowances.[15]

Such liberal programs do of course provide decent incomes for non-work, but only to those already in entrenched positions of market power. It is clearly not the beneficence of the major steel companies that explains their generous SUB, retirement, and vacation plans.

Both UC and SUB are encouraged by our tax laws. UC is a federal and state tax levied on payrolls. And SUB contributions are deductible items in corporate income taxes.

An adequate and universal guaranteed annual income would eliminate the need for the UC program and for a federally subsidized SUB. If employees, or generous employers, wish to set up a saving fund for future contingencies of non-work, they should be allowed to do so. At least we should not actively discourage such efforts of self-denial or good will. But neither should we subsidize them by tax deductibility.

DEATH TAXES

Some form of an industrial feudalism, where position, title, and status are defined by inheritance, are very real possibilities if two recent trends continue unchecked: the increasing concentration in the ownership of wealth and its link to the growing dominance of large-scale industrial empires. A guaranteed annual income and a progressive personal and corporate income tax will be important checks to that development, opening, as they will, the doors of equal opportunity to share in the output of goods and services of an industrial economy. An effective tax on the transmission of accumu-

[15] Rudolph Oswald, "SUB: Closing the Wage Loss Gap," *The American Federationist*, December 1966.

lated property could also be a significant instrument of social policy to achieve these larger goals.

While accumulated property is obviously a measure of the ability to pay taxes, any realistic use of such a tax must recognize certain important limitations: First, "wealth" is very difficult to measure. It changes hands, for tax purposes, but once a generation. The total amount of wealth extant at any given time is but a small multiple of the total income and output created each year. Secondly, while accumulated property is a measure of ability to pay taxes, the property itself is not the means of effecting that payment. Further, the timing of death has no relevance for paying the taxes due.

But these are only administrative details. Property can be assessed for tax purposes, taxes can be calculated, and months or years could be allowed to pay the tax bill. If the objectives of a meaningful guaranteed annual income and a progressive tax system are in fact to be realized, then estate taxation will of necessity have to be effectively utilized. And to close the loopholes that permit a person to transfer property before death in order to escape taxation, taxes on gifts and trusts will, of course, be integrated with the basic estate tax.[16]

The really serious and controversial question will be at what rate should transfers of accumulated property be taxed. If the aim of such a tax is to slow down the concentration of accumulated wealth, then a tax could be devised to achieve this over a period of perhaps three generations. As any given inheritance is passed on to successive generations, it would be subject to successively higher tax rates. Each succeeding generation would thus have less and less of the original inheritance. And for the third generation, the only "unearned" income available would be the guaranteed annual income. Andrew Carnegie's ideal would have been realized: the millionaire would die poor—some three generations later.

[16] For a detailed analysis of these taxes, *see* Carl S. Shoup, *Federal Estate and Gift Taxes*, Washington, D.C.: The Brookings Institution, 1966.

IN CONCLUSION

Our ultimate concern is, of course, with the distribution of the total goods and services that can be produced. And a first approximation to that distribution is the distribution of money income. It is, however, only a first approximation, and is not the only measure of economic welfare since many goods and services will be distributed by techniques other than money claims. Free public education, free medical care, parks and playgrounds will be distributed irrespective of money claims. And one of our first aims should be to expand these services to all members of the community. Money income is not the sole measure of economic welfare, but it is a significant one—one which will continue to be significant for a long long time, because how and to whom money income is distributed determines what kinds of goods and services are produced.

It would be unrealistic to expect the immediate adoption of a meaningful guaranteed annual income; it would be even more unrealistic to expect sudden revisions in tax policy as outlined above. Some form of a guaranteed income will soon be tried, however, if only as a limited and experimental alternative to what Milton Friedman has termed our "rag bag" of welfare programs. As we do experiment with new forms of income distribution, we must also experiment with new concepts in tax policy. We will move into these new and untried experiments, but if we are to move with care, then the alternatives to the status quo must be carefully and critically examined. The future into which we move can be of our own making—if we will but shed some of our inherited values in favor of the newer emerging ones.

These newer values will touch on the home, education, our relations with other less developed countries, as well as the tax policies with which this paper is concerned. Taxes will continue to be used to finance public, as distinguished from, private consumption. Coordinated with government spending, taxes will continue to be used as countercyclical devices. A meaningful guaranteed annual income, however, will also require basic changes in our definition of taxable income. And we would hope that the suggestions above provide a starting point for the critical dialogue that must precede rational change.

Ultimately we will move toward that grand vision of John Stuart Mill's great society. As long ago as the middle of the nineteenth century, Mill recognized that the laws of distribution are only the product of social customs and institutions. Once the goods and services are produced, society can distribute them by any set of rules it deems wise, useful, fair, or moral, for there are no eternally natural forces that dictate the distribution of social production. The guaranteed annual income and a coordinated tax policy are but means to the realization of that goal.

SOME SOCIAL CONSEQUENCES OF A GUARANTEED INCOME

Margaret Mead

It is characteristic of modern industrial societies to establish a close relationship between the amount of work a man does and his subsistence—as well as that of his wife, his children, and perhaps also his parents. In contrast, most of the societies that the world has known have, throughout history, linked the amount and kind of work done to the subsistence of a group, rather than that of an individual. At every level of civilization it was necessary, of course, to get enough work done so that the group was provided with food. When enough work could not be done, the consequences were serious indeed. This might happen because there were too few hunters in proportion to the number of women and children who had to be fed. It happened among the Eskimo during the period after a death, when an entire group would become hopelessly entangled in some physical and religious situation that made hunting impossible. It could also happen to them between seasons, when the snow house melted and it was not yet the season to go elsewhere for another kind of hunting. But when the hunters could hunt, there was food for everyone. The lazy, the improvident, the mentally defective, and the insane were fed from the work of the vigorous, the provident, and the ambitious.

The idea that anyone should not receive basic subsistence, food, water, and shelter—so long as there was anything left to divide—is a modern savagery.

It is true that among the Eskimo, the old were sometimes abandoned at their own request when, no longer productive, they felt they were overstraining the slender resources of the group. Among food-gathering and hunting peoples, drought may sometimes force the entire group to walk many miles to a place that has in the past produced food even in time of famine. If no food is then found, and the group must travel many more miles, some of the old and weak would have to be left behind. But even when the hunters have searched hungrily for days, while the rest of the group waited just as hungrily at the camp, there was still compassion for the unfortunate. When the Bushmen of the Kalihari Desert went on such a search for food, and one of them broke a leg, the others would attempt to carry him until food was found.

So since the beginning of man's history, men have cared for other men and assured each other of the basic necessities of life. Certainly there were times when the old had to be left to die, and sometimes even the dying had to be abandoned— although this has been reported only for people whose social relationships were deteriorating. Very often, too, not all the babies born were saved. Sometimes they were not saved because they were born while a nomadic people was making a forced march to reach new grazing grounds in time to save their herds. Sometimes they were not saved because the mother already had another baby, a weakling who commanded all her care. And sometimes they were not saved because the baby born was the wrong sex to balance marriages in the next generation. But those who were allowed to live were fed.

The idea that any human being would be so cut off from all other human links that even food and shelter were denied him is a by-product of civilization. (Civilization itself was a direct consequence of man's ability to store food, build great cities, organize large areas, put armies of conquest in the field, and bring in other groups as tributary relatives and slaves.) Stated simply, with civilization and affluence for some came poverty and vagrancy for others, and such institutions as charity—through whose practice the wealthy acquired credit in heaven. With civilization there also came the beginning of poverty that was all the more bitter because it was experienced alone and not shared with other human beings. A group of Eskimo, sitting in their melting hut with no food and the lamp going out for lack of oil, was desperately unfortunate—but not poor. Poverty is the other face of affluence. The Eskimo became poor only when he encountered the European's superior technical equipment and guns, or more lately, his airplanes, radios, and tape recorders. And this poverty is experienced by the Eskimo only when he moves into the European orbit and lives on welfare. Historically, it has been common for civilizations to create poverty by bringing into their orbit people of a different subsistence style and assigning such people an inferior place within the civilization. In time, the subordinate people are no longer close enough to their former means of livelihood to revert, should the need arise, to primitive hunting and food-gathering. They become so dependent upon more complex social organizations that when these break down almost completely in times of war and famine and pestilence, descendents of once self-sufficient peoples die by the hundreds of thousands—and sometimes by the millions.

It is thus possible to regard poverty, and mass death from starvation, as by-products of civilization. But the peculiar set of ideas that accompanies the growth of industrialization belongs more to our own Western history—and here I refer to the way we have coupled the amount of work a man does to his right to remain a viable member of the human race.

It is not difficult to trace the evolution of such concepts. As industrialization developed, the poor (multiplying in rural regions that could no longer support them) crowded into the cities. Here, so long as their survival depended on their accepting any work at any price, they were welcomed as cheap labor who could keep the wheels of industry turning. The old ties these rural poor had once enjoyed with extended kin, the neighborliness of villages, the protective largesse they had been able to count on from the manor, the castle, and the monastery—all these were swept away. The right to exist became associated with the willingness to do any kind of work that was available. This brings one to a point historians are still debating, and perhaps will argue for years to come. What is the relationship between the Protestant ethic—the insistence on work and a postponement of pleasure, as a condition of acceptability to God—and the industrial and technological development in Northern and Western Europe? There is no doubt that the two went hand in hand. In a sense, the relative poverty of the Mediterranean countries (which did not share fully all the benefits of the Industrial Revolution) may be regarded as more endurable. For it was still a shared poverty: from their pitifully inadequate supplies, the poor gave food to those who were hungrier than they.

In the United States, the unremitting demand for cheap labor meant that almost everywhere and almost all the time, the poor could survive without benefit of either the old type of kin ties and institutionalized religious charity, or the local work house provision for the needy. European countries began to experiment with various sorts of social insurance, designed to replace on a governmental basis the older forms of responsibility for the needy. But the United States ignored such social reforms and was able to survive until the Great Depression with only such simple laws as England had invented by the end of the Middle Ages for the care of the occasional needy old man or old woman, or unadoptable orphan. The United States was able to do this because this country still offered virtually untapped resources and vast amounts of free land to a population growing in numbers through immigration as well as natural increase.

Essentially, our ethic was as harsh as that which prevailed in England during the early days of the Industrial Revolution, or in Ireland, during the potato famine. Yet it seemed less harsh because of the sense of space and opportunity, which was so integral a part of early American life. The sense of wider spaces into which everyone was free to move, and a faith that opportunity waited just around the corner, was instilled into Americans. It did not matter whether he was a three-generation native living in a log cabin where the wind whistled through the chinks while pine logs provided a bright blaze, or a recent immigrant packed into the noisome slums of New York City's Lower East Side. American school children learned to recite verses celebrating Opportunity, which claimed:

> They do me wrong who say I come no more
> When once I knock and fail to find you in;
> For everyday I stand outside your door
> And bid you wake, and rise to fight and win.[1]

Or this:

> Master of human destinies am I!
> Fame, love, and fortune on my footsteps wait.
> Cities and fields I walk; I penetrate
> Deserts and seas remote, and passing by
> Hovel and mart and palace—soon or late
> I knock unbidden once at every gate!
> If sleeping, wake—if feasting, rise before
> I turn away. It is the hour of fate,
> And they who follow me reach every state
> Mortals desire, and conquer every foe
> Save death; but those who doubt or hesitate,
> Condemned to failure, penury, and woe,
> Seek me in vain and uselessly implore.
> I answer not, and I return no more![2]

The Great Depression challenged, for the first time, the belief that if any man were willing to work, he could find work to do. It challenged the belief that if any man could not feed himself and his family, it was because he simply was not willing to work at *anything*. Although the Great Depression did bring in legislation that provided minimum insurance against starvation for most Americans, it did not truly change

---

[1] Walter Malone, "Opportunity," in *The Best Loved Poems of the American People,* ed. Hazel Felleman, (Garden City, N.Y.: Doubleday, 1936), pp. 100–1.
[2] John James Ingalls, "Opportunity," in *Poems That Live Forever,* ed. Hazel Felleman (Garden City, N.Y.: Doubleday, 1965), pp. 411–12.

the attitudes that prevailed before the Depression. Not only do these attitudes still prevail, they are today complicated by three generations of families who have endured the humiliations and deteriorations of our present system of welfare.

We still employ the workhouse psychology of Tudor England. We will take care of those within our gates when we must, at least to the point of preventing death from starvation, or seeing that lack of shoes does not keep a child from attending school. But we resent any increase, by migration or birth, of those who must be cared for by the people of our city or our town. And we resent a corollary fact—that there are today many essential services that go unperformed because no one can be found to do the work, and this at the very time when so many are on welfare.

Historically, we are a country where the eager immigrant turned his hand to any task at any wage. We have never really adjusted to the combination of a legal minimum wage and an unemployment insurance policy that insists only that a man should find the kind of work he is trained to do. This combination is even more difficult to accept since it co-exists with a welfare system that will continue to support the unemployed engineer, insurance salesman, or truck driver when their unemployment insurance runs out—even though there are plenty of dishwashing jobs that need to be done.

The American ethic, shaped in the styles of the open frontier and the land of golden opportunity for the determined immigrant, had its peculiar imperatives. It insisted that a man, no matter what his status, should be willing to turn his hand to any task. It insisted that the newcomer to our country, or a region of our country, should be willing to begin afresh, at any level. The traditional respect for the man of humble beginnings perpetuates this feeling. So does the fact that in the United States, maturity for a man is essentially economic. When a man can support himself in a manner that includes the support of his wife and children, he is counted a man. If he loses his job after marriage and must again be supported by his parents in their home, as happened to so many men during the Depression, he temporarily returns to the status of a minor—a status he may leave by again becoming economically independent. The American belief that maturity is reversible played a role in a mayoralty campaign not many decades ago, which was based on the threat that King George was again about to take over the United States, presumably because we were not doing too well economically.[3]

Of course, we have not really abandoned any of our essential beliefs. We still believe that it is wrong for a man, or an unmarried woman, not to be gainfully employed. The rich man who makes token trips to a brokerage house, or engages in politics, may be making only symbolic gestures, from the standpoint of the relationship between his income and his earnings—but he has to make them. We still believe that there is something wrong if a man is supported by his parents after he completes graduate or postgraduate training, however well they are able to support him. And students, anxious to escape the dependent position of being supported (and controlled) by their families, accept support from their wives —only to find that this transforms their wives into parent figures to be abandoned when degrees are obtained. Uncounted hundreds of thousands of families live on less than they are entitled to in terms of present welfare concepts, because they still insist upon being self-respecting, self-supporting persons. Meanwhile, those who advocate that we control the right of the poor to have children point with horror to the fact that families in which fathers do have jobs still need welfare help. In their view, the right to marry and have children is inextricably involved with the right to act and live as a mature man, and is based on total economic and social self-sufficiency.

This genuinely pioneer view was made obsolete long ago by the urbanization of the country. But by extension, we also deny mature status to students, who are not considered to

[3] For girls, maturity is attained by either marriage or by economic independence, and so presents a different problem.

be earning a living, no matter how hard they may be working to prepare themselves for a career essential to our economy. We still treat them as sub-citizens, whatever their age. The scholarships and fellowships we extend to them are based on a means test and treated like a dole. University students often find difficulties in renting a home, getting a telephone, or voting—rights that are accorded to an economically self-sufficient high school dropout working at the lowest-level job.

A further expression of the American ethic that a man should work his way up, should begin at the bottom of the ladder, and should be willing to begin over and over again is found in our treatment of young Americans who grow up "too fast" (this was the perspicacious comment of a woman juror in the first trial of Alger Hiss). We have small sympathy for those who fail to pass through the appropriate apprenticeship stages in any occupation—stages that by common agreement we make difficult. Each stage in education demands that students begin all over again, as "freshmen" targets for upper classmen hazing. The young man who completes a professional degree must begin again at the lowest rung of the ladder, and nothing is more dangerous to academic success than to omit such stages. Deans and heads of departments carefully balance the amount of suffering at each stage; those who have not endured the proper amount of suffering cannot compensate by pointing to their research work or different experience.

The convention that the good immigrant takes whatever he can get and makes his own way—once applied to peasants coming in droves to the United States—continued to be applied to the highly educated refugees from Europe, throughout the Hitler period of the 1930s and early 1940s, and even to some of the refugees after the Hungarian uprising in 1956. Educated men, while being given hospitality by their economic peers, were still expected to accept menial jobs at once, while they laid plans to resume their professions.

The demands that we make on those who have inadequate

education, health, motivation, or opportunity help to perpetuate an ethic in which subsistence is inextricably tied to a paid job, except for retired persons, married women, or widows and spinsters living on the accumulated savings of some man's previous earnings. And this ethic insidiously encourages the belief that if people didn't *have* to work, they wouldn't. All proposals for a guaranteed annual income, however phrased, conjure up, on the one hand, the loss of independence and autonomy, and on the other hand, an army of people living on welfare, without the slightest interest in taking jobs that are waiting to be filled. Work, to be work, must be a duty, and not a pleasure. Rich and poor alike are seen as being goaded by a variety of pressures into doing some work, and all are believed anxious to do as little as possible.

We have been unable to revise our ethic fast enough to fit our changing condition. The unadorned truth is that we do not need now, and will not need later, much of the marginal labor—the very young, the very old, the very uneducated, and the very stupid. This fact continues to go unrecognized as we talk about "full employment." The temporary stringencies of a wartime situation obscure the fact that our economy will need fewer workers per unit of output with every year that passes. The old need for cheap labor is fast disappearing, and with it the ability to coerce people into taking ill-paid, unsafe, and low-level jobs by the physical threat of starvation, and the psychological threat of a loss of self-respect and autonomy. As minimum wage laws go into effect, machinery simply replaces human cotton pickers in the Southeast—and New York and Chicago have more mouths to feed. The motive power of the need for self-respect does not act on the new migrants to the cities as it acted upon our pioneer ancestors, and upon the recent wave of highly motivated immigrants from other lands. People who have lived a marginal life of peonage and dependency in unicrop economies, where the gains from production and consumption were both drained away from their lives, have not been schooled in a major commitment to autonomy. They want to eat. If these migrations had occurred at a time when society was still willing to starve them into working, and then pay them starvation wages, the results would undoubtedly be different. But today we are caught in the midst of a half-realized ethical revolution; we are too rich and conspicuously affluent to bear to use starvation as a weapon. Yet we are too tradional-minded to realize the drastic revisions we will have to make to bring our social expectation in line with the facts of our changing technology.

Like all colonial peoples, we have attempted to preserve certain elements from our ancestral culture. These ways of thinking and being tend to continue despite new situations to which they are inappropriate. Such discrepancies between the ethic and the reality have been maintained for hundreds of years. We can be forced to examine our ancient premises by crisis or threat of crisis—such as is now presented by pollution of the human environment, by the chaotic state of the inner cores of our large cities, by the population explosion, and by the need to readjust our methods of distribution to fit changes in production that are the concomitants of automation.

Since the changes in our distribution patterns will have to be made by the federal government, the revision in our ethic must necessarily be nationwide. Glaring contradictions result when a government policy is inadequately supported by discussion on a nationwide level. All through the late 1930s and 1940s, for example, children studying history were not taught anything of the events that took place in this country after 1932. This period was neglected on the assumption that as soon as a Republican administration came in, it would, of course, sweep away all the New Deal legislation—so why bother to teach it?

We may feel a kind of dependence upon, and expect to give loyalty to, our own locality, our state, or our country. But the view of a nation cross-cut with regional administrative lines (so real to the special Washington office of the agency involved) has no reality for the country. Each attempt to assume greater federal responsibility is fought as an increase in bureaucratization. Those who advocate federal responsibility for slum clearance, schools, or welfare in one area of the country will fight against it in another area where the same conditions prevail. They will do so in the face of the obvious inability of localities with very different resources to cope equally with a national burden.

For these reasons, when we discuss the possible effects of some form of guaranteed annual income, we must do so in terms that have meaning for the nation, and that can be disseminated by the nationwide news-dispensing networks.

As we have accepted the right of every resident in the United States to a minimum of subsistence help—however inadequate and niggardly it often is, and however grudgingly it is given—it will be necessary to accept some extension of this principle. As the people of the nation take the burden from the people in small towns, poor cities, and needy states, new definitions of responsibility will be required. Unless these responsibilities are defined in terms meaningful to the entire nation, they will be successfully fought and evaded. It may be argued that the cost of the undeclared Vietnam war and the increased draft quotas are so deeply resented because the nation as a whole is not involved in the war. In an all-out war we have the greatest awareness of ourselves as a nation, and the least resentment of Washington. Yet, in a situation of total war, people not only have to contribute resources, labor, and military service, but also want to contribute to the outcome of the struggle. A guaranteed annual income would provide the same kind of total involvement—not only would everyone be taxed, but everyone would be involved personally as a participant. Both contributing to, and receiving, a guaranteed annual income could and should be viewed as greater participation in the life of the nation.

It is therefore necessary to see first how a guaranteed annual income would affect the definition of citizenship in the United States. At the present time, citizenship is an internationally oriented concept; it is something that birth in the United States confers, as compared with the citizenship conferred or imposed by birth in other countries. American citizenship is seen as something that natives of other countries may acquire, but also as something that Americans, both new and old, for example, can lose by serving in the armed forces of another country. It gives one the right to a passport and to protection abroad. Also, there are a lot of things that someone who is not a citizen cannot do—notably, work in governmental contexts of any sort, or receive scholarships and grants designed for Americans. But whenever he is home in the United States, the American feels only a weak relationship between his citizenship and his sense of participation in the nation. This has been accentuated by attempts of the extreme right, and sometimes the extreme left, to promote their partisan causes by the use of nationwide identifications and American historical symbols. Thinking in nationwide terms has almost become confined to extreme ideological positions.

If one interviews Americans about the domestic implications of being an American, one sometimes gets vague and general answers about how good it is to live in a free country or in a country with such a high standard of living. Sometimes the respondent is quite specific, giving particulars about being glad that he is not a citizen of some other country "living under a dictator," or how he can "get a job with the city," in contrast with the non-citizen, who cannot. Significantly, it is not the individual citizen who makes widest use of American symbols, but those groups, whether left or right, who are either concerned with importing a "foreign ideology" or preventing its importation.

If we are to have a guaranteed annual income, it is clear that it must be inclusive, and it must apply either to every citizen, or to every resident. If it is seen as the opposite face of taxation, then as foreign residents are taxed like American citizens, the all-inclusive category should be *resident*. Those who live here, and are taxed here, share together in the benefits a rich and productive country is able to assure every adult member of the society and, directly or indirectly, all children. Whether citizenship or residence is the criterion, we may have to deal with the problems of immigration. We must answer the question of whether such recognition of full participation in a society, still nationally bounded, is compatible with the same kind of hospitality that prevailed when the country needed cheap labor. This earlier condition, combined with our tradition of giving religious and political refuge, has left us as residue a certain amount of hospitality, even in today's world.

If we are to avoid the psychology of the English Tudor town, where the sick stranger was carried out into the fields to die, so that the town would not have the expense of burying him, we will need some way of reconciling the freedom to come here with the freedom to live here and share in a guaranteed annual income. And we shall need to develop an ethic based on generosity and a sense of affluence and abundant resources. In time, there will be fewer tendencies toward limiting what we can give to others, because we have given so much to ourselves. At present, however, it might be well to stress how the well-being of the country would be served by a guaranteed annual income that would stabilize the economy by ensuring it a steady group of consumers. It would help the picture if immigrants are seen as valuable consumers, as once they were seen as valuable in the production process. The total economy can be stimulated, through the development and use of machines, to meet the needs of the new consumers. If these measures were taken, then we could work on other major stabilizing mechanisms such as establishing the best ratio of men to land, and controlling the growth of metropolitan clusters.

What would be the consequences of a guaranteed annual income? It is apparent that its impact on different groups in the population would vary enormously. The first impact would be upon men of wage-earning age. (The position of the retired has already been drastically altered by social security and medicare; the position of children will be a function of the changed position of adults.)

There is an increasing tendency for young men to assert their maturity by marriage and fatherhood. But when such actions are combined with economic dependency, they are excused only if the young husband and father is a student or is obtaining further training. To be a respected member of American society, a man must earn a living and provide the major part of the support of his wife and children. In the same context, the money he earns should be enough to keep them all; any money his wife may earn should be complementary, but not primary. (So strong is this feeling that many men are unwilling to have their wives work, for fear someone will think they have to work—and this would impugn their own capabilities as mature men.) This belief that a real man can support his family all alone is of course shared by women. To the degree that a wife has to support her husband and children, she loses respect for her husband's manhood. Among the urban proletariat of all racial attributions, the inability of the men to get jobs reduces their effectiveness as husbands and fathers. This has a variety of implications that have recently been spelled out in many analyses of lower class family structure. But some of the older consequences have not been as fully spelled out, as, for example, in the mechanics of gang formation among boys in the slum areas of American cities. In such areas, the normal American socialization pattern—in which the parents are audience to the exploits and successes of the child—is lacking, because the father lacks the respect of his children. The boy with leadership qualities, robbed of the adult audience he would normally enjoy, turns to younger boys for his audience, becomes a gang leader, and by so doing seals himself off from the normal paths of advancement in American life.

Our discussions about the weakness of family ties in urban slums (often directly counterpointed to the strength of such ties in the same population before migration from the rural South, rural Puerto Rico, or Ireland) has not been correctly focused. It has dwelt almost entirely on the weaknesses in the family structure, rather than upon the essentially economic nature of those weaknesses. If men—in a society that has defined its men as providers—are unable to provide either money or services to support their families, the family structure breaks down. Then we get the fatherless families, the ADC mothers, and the adolescents who face a difficult and often devastating choice. They must decide whether to play the role their fathers should have played, and help support their mothers, or by rebelling against this position, to assume instead the role their fathers are actually playing—a role of dependency and irresponsibility.

A guaranteed annual income would provide such fathers with an ability they once had in rural areas but have forfeited by failure to find jobs in the city—the simple ability to provide for their families. Their relationship to their wives and children would be stabilized at the center. Their manhood, instead of being called to question, would be reaffirmed. From this stability, they could go on to look for forms of employment from which they could hope to improve their position—now that they had a position capable of being improved. This kind of stabilization is urgent and imperative, unless we wish by some means to attempt to dissociate the father from any provision of a livelihood for the family, and reduce his role to that of the mother's partner in sex and procreation. Welfare, doled out so that his wife and children will not starve, is an incentive to absenteeism and parasitism. (One cannot anticipate very much success for the efforts of those who would have welfare agencies treat the matter more sympathetically, and who insist that any sex partner of the wife be allowed to share her home—so as to contribute social, if not economic, stability.)

At present, it is difficult to predict whether a guaranteed annual income for presently resourceless families might increase their fecundity. To the extent that the men were stimulated to add to their small reliable subsistence incomes, this should not be the case. To the extent that absolute hopelessness encourages a resort to the one fully human power left to the poor, reproductivity, a decrease in despair should provide a check on reproduction. To the extent that middle class models continue to emphasize large families as the perquisite of affluence, there might be a positive relationship with the family size of those men who were stimulated to greater effort by the provision of basic security, and a negative relationship where a guaranteed annual income was taken as adequate and no need was seen to make any further effort. A relationship between ambition and larger families would not in itself be evil, and could be corrected by changing trends in middle class ideals about family size.

The greatest effects of a guaranteed annual income on individual and family stability might be expected to appear among the most recent migrants to the large cities. These new migrants have not yet lost a style of life in which men who provide for the family in other ways than earning money are nevertheless respected. The smallest effects might be expected among those who had lived in either urban or rural slums for two or more generations, and among whom responsible behavior patterns for men are lacking. There is probably no justification in any claim that a guaranteed annual income will do anything more for such people than to substitute a more bearable, less expensive, and more dignified form of welfare. But their children would be on a better basis with other children—not separated by a gap because of the source of their income.

In the lower middle class, the guaranteed annual income would make itself felt most by relating the members of the middle class to the rest of society. It would reaffirm the fact that their comfortable way of life is related to the prosperity and productivity of the country, and not simply to their own virtuous industriousness and saving habits. Also, as many new middle class families actually have no savings, and live on an essentially lower class pattern of installment buying, a guaranteed annual income would provide this group with a greater sense of security. In so doing, it would convert them into more stable citizens, less suspicious of their own community and their nation. The anxiety that goes with fear of losing a job is greater in the middle class, where the idea of not having work is inconceivably awful, than among the very poor. The special provision for Committed Spending that would cushion the effects of loss of expected salary level, as well as dealing merely with immediate job loss, becomes particularly important for those who have saved and planned and are then confronted with the types of unemployment that accompany technological changes and large-scale reorganizations.

This is so even in the upper middle class. Here I include the professional and upper managerial groups, highly motivated and able individuals who have reached their present status by consistent effort, often combined with large amounts of familial support. This is not a group with whom we ordinarily associate the kind of insecurity with which the Guaranteed Annual Income is designed to cope. Nevertheless, in today's fluid, rapidly changing world, it is particularly members of middle management and liaison who are most seriously endangered. In the United States, it is possible to identify a new class of the previously successful who, sometimes in early middle age, are bypassed in the course of social change, with long compulsory periods before new and even partially satisfactory employment is found. Committed Spending will make it easier for them to make such transitions and reduce the sense of bitterness and injustice that now characterizes many of those who find themselves suddenly in transition, where they had expected continuous promotion and success.

Although the upper middle class is characteristically motivated far beyond considerations of immediate economic gain, sharing a core of security with workers whose industriousness they have so often questioned should have ethical significance. Many of the upper middle class already work many more hours than their contracts call for. But even for these, it will make it easier to know that their less fortunate classmates and associates are not being forced summarily into sudden violent reorganizations of every aspect of their lives, and to know that they live in a country where not only no one is hungry, but where no one is demeaned. The extra economic efforts, which are almost an automatic accompaniment of middle class status today, will be played in a wider context.

The small but important upper class in the United States has always been faced with a society lacking a responsible role for its fortunate elite—a society that presented its upper class with nowhere to go but down. There has been no consistent, continuous role for members of our upper class families. There has been the additional handicap that they belonged to families and not to a nationwide class. It is not yet clear whether a guaranteed annual income can be made to give them a new sense of freedom of choice. But a society in which all occupations are followed by choice, and none by threat of starvation, is intrinsically closer to an aristocratic ideal of responsibility.

Now we may turn to women, and consider the effects upon them. Are women, upon becoming adults, to be given a guaranteed annual income just as would be given to a man, and then suddenly disenfranchised and reduced to dependency level if they marry? This seems to be our present trend. Single women are increasingly treated as individuals in terms of jobs, protective legislation, and social benefits, but those who marry are no longer treated in the same way. We are fast approaching a stage in which married women can, in a sense, be compared only to nuns in the Middle Ages—set apart, subject to separate rules, and condemned to physical labor as a condition of following a chosen way of life. Women who are not married are treated as responsible individuals and presumably might be given a guaranteed annual income just as any mature man would be. If they had any dependents, as so many women do, these could be treated as the dependents of a man are treated. (This is not so at present, where, for example, a man is permitted to take his wife overseas, but a spinster does not have the same permission to take a mother or a dependent sister or niece.)

The decision as to whether women should be treated as full individuals, married or not, would be a crucial one. Giving them such status would conflict with many of the articulated motivations in favor of a guaranteed annual income, such as reinforcing the manliness of men and preserving the family. The dependency of the wife has been such a significant element in our idea of the family that it will be difficult to substitute a status for women based on choice rather than on economic advantage. If, on reaching majority, each woman were to be assured a guaranteed annual income for life, and given the same security as her brother, both instituting and continuing in marriage would be matters of free choice. The status of a family would be that of two adults, freely joined to rear their children together. The standard of living would be calculated on the contribution of two adults to each family, and the family would not be dependent upon some archaic survival of a theory that two can live almost as cheaply as one. As we have adapted to the idea of women working, partly due to the rising standard of living and partly to an insistent demand for cheaper educated labor, we have merely substituted work outside the home plus domestic drudgery for total economic dependency. So, today, the demands made on a married woman who works outside the home are almost impossible to meet. If all women, married or not married, had a guaranteed annual income, we might expect to see fewer mothers of young children working outside the home and consequently far fewer unsupervised and uncared-for children, overworked mothers, irresponsible husbands and fathers, and women aging before their time from carrying a double load. We might expect, if women, married or unmarried, were given a guaranteed annual income, that fewer married women would work full time, and that perhaps more of them would work part time as choice replaced coercion.

The effect on the young adult, male or female, would perhaps be the most striking. At present, the social worker is plagued with a series of discrepancies. Neither boys nor girls are really welcome at home after they have reached physical maturity. In the social classes where they can afford to go away to college, they survive in an uneasy dependency—sometimes even after their own marriages. But where they must live at home, whether they work or continue in college, an overwhelming proportion of young adults are pushed toward marriage as an escape. This results in premature parenthood, too heavy a load on young men who attempt both to support a family and to obtain further training, and often also in too-large families. At present, service in the armed forces is the only other escape for young men, and there is no other escape for the girl who cannot go away to school. There are also further contradictions in our demand that young people continue in school, as a service to their country, and in our refusal to pay them for doing so. While boys who are out of school perform unskilled and trivial tasks and are paid as men, students are submitted to a means test, and the best fellowship available for the most gifted student is not supposed to equal what he would earn "if he worked." Parents who can possibly afford it are still supposed to finance their children through college.

There is a tremendous discrepancy between the possibilities of support in higher education for those who early make a career choice, and for those students who are slow in settling on one particular career line rather than another—yet some of those who are slow to decide will later be our most valuable thinkers. Only with affluent parents behind them, do they have much chance for the kind of exploratory educational period they require. If each young man and woman reaching eighteen years of age had his or her own guaranteed annual income, then the questions of education, work, and marriage would fall into place entirely as matters of choice. To facilitate that choice further, we might also initiate some system of nationwide service that would acquaint young people with the possibilities for different kinds of careers in different parts of our country and the world.

Today we are not able to support our artists, our composers, our poets. The richest nation the world has ever known has a handful of scholarships, a miserable little collection of prizes and grants. It offers its gifted individuals nothing except a chance to work at some other occupation and give the time left over to the arts. With a guaranteed annual income, young people would be able to spend the time necessary to perfect their skills. It would put an end to composers becoming night watchmen, and poets trying to support themselves as silk-screen craftsmen. This support would be their right, as it would for any other citizen, and would not have to be debated as a matter of patronage. A poet, like anyone else, would have a right to subsistence and the right to choose to do something unremunerative the rest of the time.

For this is the crux of the matter—the right to choose to spend one's life in a way that society does not remunerate. In certain stages of industrialization, especially before the introduction of automation, every hand was needed to produce and to build up capital goods. It was not possible to encourage "unproductive activities" in societies still struggling to industrialize. Where this is so the arts must be subsidized if they are to survive, as in the countries of Eastern Europe, and to some extent fettered by the state. But where there is no longer a shortage of labor, this need not be the case.

To free the arts, we should have to exorcise the belief that it is morally dangerous for anyone to choose to do nothing—that is, to choose not to make money. This belief has been terribly strong, and it has been reinforced by the low level of opportunities available to fill the growing leisure of the formerly overworked classes—people who never had a chance to develop taste or skill. To learn to believe that leisure can be a good part of life, and that it can be filled with activities of a high artistic, social, or spiritual nature, will require both a change in belief and a change in the opportunities that are available. There must be a substitution of a great deal of locally based activity for the present mass-produced recreation. But to have good little theaters, for example, there must be many people who are free to devote their time to building and developing them. Guaranteed annual income would provide for this.

The twin of our belief that time not spent in gainful employment will corrupt the soul is our fear that if men are not coerced by threats of ignominy and dire poverty, they will not work. In such a case, it is believed that all the dull, unpleasant, routine, and degrading tasks that must be done, will not be done. It is undoubtedly true that if a man does not live under dire threat, he will ask more of his job. He will not tolerate unsafe working conditions, a degrading work situation, a job that defines him as less than human. Members of minority groups will refuse to accept jobs that are defined as appropriate only for those of low status. Factory work once liberated men, and particularly women, from the domestic drudgery in which they had neither dignity nor rights. This trend, which has already gone very far in the United States, would be accelerated with a guaranteed annual income. No one would accept work in which human rights are disregarded. Every task would have to be made worth doing, if it were to be done at all. Every task would have to provide some desired reward, a fair return in money, good working conditions, a sense of purpose, dignity, and participation.

We will have to give up the belief that men work only for money, and realize that men also work to do something together, to have a purpose in life—a purpose that is provided for the mother of young children by her home and that an increasing number of older married women now demand also. Idleness as a full-time occupation produces dullness and ennui, and people can be trained to put up with it only by the most extreme measures—such as certain kinds of compulsory military service, imprisonment, or hospitalization. But also we have to see that necessary tasks are fit to do. If everything that can be done by a machine is done by a machine, and work itself is necessary and remunerative, dignified and safe, there is no reason to believe that the majority of Americans, deeply committed to the possibilities of bettering themselves, will not elect to work. Of course, all such work must be remunerated above the guaranteed annual income. A man would not give up his guaranteed annual income when he worked, but would simply supplement it; in the case of those who made large salaries, the guaranteed annual income would be counted against taxes.

In Britain after World War II, it was difficult to raise production because the workers had everything they had learned to want that it was possible for the country to provide. As a result, they simply refused to work overtime. They would have worked for better housing, but this was not a practical possibility. This is not the case in the United States. A people to whom moonlighting is almost second nature would not abstain from work and live on a subsistence level. A United States with a guaranteed annual income would be a United States of tremendous productivity—a total population with a guaranteed annual income would assure an enormous and steady mass market, and a continual output of more and more desirable goods and associated services. People would, as some of those on welfare do now, refuse jobs that had neither good pay nor interest nor social importance to recommend them. We have had to pay school janitors more than teachers to get the jobs done. We have had to glamorize the role of the airline hostess to get well-educated and responsible girls to combine high responsibility with the daily performance of onerous, menial tasks. The fact that good restaurants fail to get waitresses while girls compete for the airplane hostess jobs is simply a comment on the way waitresses are exploited in restaurants. It does not point to any inherent unwillingness to work on the part of those who quit. A poor job cannot encourage those who have experienced a long and demoralizing life among others who were also on welfare to strive for self-realization. But we need not argue from this—from the boy on the corner who refuses five dollars to shovel some snow—to any fear that in a society where subsistence is a right of every citizen, rich or poor, the provision of such subsistence would make people unwilling to work.

There would be those who found the guaranteed annual income sufficient and went fishing, or painted pictures, or devoted themselves to some form of religious work. There would, undoubtedly, be those who drank it up, or gambled it away, or who spent their days at the races or their nights in the numbers racket. Large mass societies, like much smaller and simpler societies, have not learned how to bring up every child so that he or she will fit into the adult world, instead of into some illegal and disapproved nook that is also provided. But the danger that we shall be underwriting the failures of skid row is trivial compared with the benefits the guaranteed annual income would give us. It would provide dignity for every citizen and choice for every citizen. It would free us from the stigma of poverty and the demoralization of welfare, and turn our affluence from a reproach into a point of pride among nations.

CONTINUING EDUCATION AND BASIC ECONOMIC SECURITY

A. A. Liveright[1]

IMPLICATIONS OF A LIFE OF FREEDOM FROM WANT

Basic Economic Security in the most rudimentary form is already with us, and has been for a long time. Most communities provide subsistence for those who have no income, while a growing number of Americans live on social security and other forms of pensions. The Basic Economic Security proposal made by Theobald and others would change the situation significantly, however, in that it would establish by national policy and legislation the individual's right to a minimum income.

The necessity for establishing Basic Economic Security lies in the efficient machines we have created, which can now do many tasks formerly requiring workers, and which will soon be able to replace millions more workers at all levels in the economy as suggested by Irving Kaplan in the initial article. At the same time these machines will be capable of prodigious output, so that the link between labor and production will no longer exist.

In an economy that can produce abundance it is obviously unnecessary for people to live in want. Recognizing that the increasing productivity of the economy can result in a state of increased affluence for all, Basic Economic Security would provide a floor below which incomes would not fall.

Committed Spending is another proposal to make the technological revolution less painful, by continuing the incomes of employees whose jobs are eliminated. It is related to the ideas of severance pay, early retirement, and other plans now

[1] The author is indebted to Mrs. Kenneth Haygood for her assistance in revising and editing this chapter.

in existence for providing more than subsistence income to those who can no longer be employed.

These ideas are proposed now as practical solutions to problems that are already with us. They also point out dramatically the fact that we have embarked upon our journey to the world of machine-produced abundance, and that there is no turning back. Slowly at first, and now with accelerating speed, we are moving toward a time when many people may have no need, and indeed no opportunity, to hold paid jobs, and this will be a revolution in a world in which identity, status, and self-esteem are often determined by a person's job.

There will be considerable unevenness in the way in which this change takes place. Professionals and academicians may find themselves working more, while technicians and clerks do not have to work at all. But eventually the life of abundance should provide more leisure for all, and the opportunity to choose interests and activities that will lead to a life of satisfaction.

Several implications for continuing education are to be found in these developments.

The first is the increased number of people who will have time for educational activities and who will need new sources of interest and reward.

The second is the need to shift the emphasis in continuing education from job-linked programs to the development of the individual and his environment.

The third is the need for extensive action in teaching people about cybernation and its effects, and in educating them to exercise responsible control over the extent, the pace, and the way in which we will permit machines to affect our lives. Machines must be made to serve man, and not the reverse.

Fourth, we must expand our notion of work to cover many community, service, artistic, and volunteer activities that have value for society and that could be reorganized to provide recognition and rewards in somewhat the same way that income-producing jobs do now.

Fifth, if a life of learning is to be possible for all, we must decide on a fair allocation of the work that remains to be done. Shall the young mother continue unaided in the rearing of the children, and shall doctors continue to work long hours when others are free to pursue their individual interests?

Sixth, adult education must build toward a society that is not only technologically advanced and economically secure, but also one that is more civilized and humane. We must seek out the means by which man himself may be improved, intellectually and morally.

Seventh, we must undertake now to educate our citizens and our leaders to base their decisions more on objective and realistic appraisal of the situation, and less on faith and hunch. The resources of technology make it possible to consider vast stores of information when choosing alternatives, and the far-reaching consequences of our domestic and international decisions make it imperative that we develop more effective procedures for arriving at them.

These implications will be discussed in the following pages.

THE USES OF LEISURE

Through the ages men have sought, and some have achieved, security and leisure. Until now these have been an elite, and they have used their freedom from work to seek fulfillment in many ways. They have studied, traveled, contemplated, composed music, poetry, and prose; they have become sportsmen, or philanderers or religious, or sought after a happiness described by Edith Hamilton in *The Greek Way* as "the exercise of vital powers along the lines of excellence in a life affording them scope." Cybernation may help the Western world achieve this ancient dream by making possible security for all and leisure to pursue happiness, each according to his dream.

But leisure, while it has been sought and cherished, can

also be dreary and demoralizing. If leisure brings an end to interesting activity and valued relationships, and if it involves loss of status, it will not be viewed as a blessing. Workers who have been retired unwillingly reject their leisure as being "out of things." The unemployed wish they "had something to do." These groups, who in our society actually do have basic economic security, find that this is not enough. Many other needs are present, which are also satisfied in the work situation. Social needs and the opportunity for achievement and recognition are some of these, and if work is no longer available, our non-work activities will have to be so directed as to provide for them.

An attractive alternative to a life in which the major focus is work could combine inquiry and learning; the practice of an art or craft; participation in politics, church and community affairs; service to others through hospitals, youth groups, or social service agencies; recreation, travel, and social activities; and a host of other enjoyable and meaningful pursuits.

All of these alternatives require that resources must be made available to enable people to study and learn, to develop skills, and to expand their capacities in the most rewarding ways.

OBSTACLES TO THE ACCEPTANCE OF THE LEARNING SOCIETY

1. People who need continuing education most are least likely to be able to take advantage of it. Those who now participate in adult education programs are mostly young, relatively well educated, and in the middle income range. Those who have leisure now are older people; many of them are poorly educated and have scanty means. Among these are such groups as former Studebaker employees and packinghouse workers, who lost their jobs after many years of employment in the same line of work. Attempts to retrain these

workers for other jobs have been unsuccessful and it is clear that our present programs are not adequate to work effectively with such groups.

2. The rewards and incentives in our society are mostly job-connected, and there is a moral value attached to work itself. These values and incentives contribute greatly to the individual's self-image, so that to be unable to have a job has destructive effects on his confidence and self-esteem.

3. The kind of education that is needed to prepare people to accept changes in values is the kind we know least about. In spite of increasing knowledge in scientific and behavioral fields, we have been slow to develop effective means for changing antisocial and self-destructive values into socially constructive ones.

4. Although the new technology could be used to expand and innovate in education, it has been developed primarily to serve industry and defense. For example, our use of computers for information storage and retrieval in education lags far behind their use in business, although they are "natural" tools for study and research.

5. It is often very difficult for an adult to find out what programs are available. No agency in any community takes responsibility for providing information about the continuing education activities in which the residents may participate, and there is no national directory or source book listing opportunities for independent study. Registration requirements are often forbidding, and facilities frequently are inappropriate. The motivations that bring adults to continuing education programs are rarely taken account of when curricula for adults are planned.

6. The emphasis on youth in our society causes us to give low priority to continuing adult education. Resources, research, and interest in education have been concentrated on youth, to the neglect of lifelong learning. We do little to educate the generation now in leadership positions, and whose actions influence the course of the future.

7. The little continuing education available is largely designed to serve vocational, occupational, and professional needs. Of the twenty-five million students of adult education in 1962, 32 per cent were in vocationally oriented programs. Almost all federal funds for adult education are for job-related programs, while in many less affluent countries governments support humanistic education for adults.

SIGNS OF PROGRESS TOWARD LIFELONG LEARNING

Despite the bleak picture painted in the foregoing section, signs of progress are also present. Indeed, some of the negative aspects have within them the seeds of hope. Among these positive elements are the following:

1. Despite the overwhelming emphasis on jobs and work, there is a growing acceptance of learning, the learner, the teacher, and the intellectual. Greater importance is now attached to scientific thinking and research, including pure research, and an increasingly better educated population is coming to regard education as the key to the "good life." A recent Harris poll reported that for Americans the major area of dissatisfaction was the desire for more education.

2. Many Americans do succeed in their pursuit of continuing education. In 1962 twenty-five million people were engaged in some kind of adult education, and nine million of these were involved in independent study, a very substantial number considering the difficulties placed in their path.

3. There has been a vast increase in participation in the arts and cultural activities. The sales of books, musical instruments, records, and objects of art have all boomed in the past ten years. The number of orchestras and art galleries has also boomed, indicating more attention to and support for artistic and cultural enterprises.

4. Increasing numbers of TV viewers are protesting the

low level of programs offered by the commercial outlets. Many of these viewers are turning to educational stations for more stimulating TV fare. At the same time the networks are devoting more attention to sound news reporting and to the telecasting of excellent documentaries.

5. The technology for exciting breakthroughs in educational materials, techniques, and equipment is already available. It is now possible, for example, to install individual learning carrels in homes, as well as in community learning and information centers. Considering the opportunities offered, these prospects are likely soon to attract the risk capital necessary for full-scale development.

6. Volunteer service alternatives to work-for-pay have already been developed and are gradually becoming accepted. The vast potential that lies in channeling people's altruistic impulses has become apparent. The Peace Corps, the Vista Volunteer program, and the Service Corps developed by retired executives for management consultation overseas suggest the ways in which volunteer service can be a challenging and rewarding activity. These newer forms, as well as the established service organizations, can offer interesting, socially useful tasks for those with increased leisure.

7. Concern with questions of personal identity and the meaning of life is manifested in the rapidly growing number of adults enrolled in courses in psychology, philosophy, foreign affairs, urban planning, and personal development. In institutions that offer imaginative programs, adults are participating in large numbers in programs of liberal education bearing no direct relationships to job or economic success.

8. Predictions that increased leisure would result in personal and family disintegration have not turned out to be true. Steelworkers have used their long vacations to work around the house, travel, and do useful non-paid work. The electrical workers of New York attend liberal education programs in facilities owned by the union. A Florida community for the retired easily passed an assessment in the community for a

continuing education program and facilities to house it. These developments lead us to believe that leisure is not as threatening and destructive as has been thought, and that people can adjust to the new goals and activities required by a new way of life.

EXPANDING POSSIBILITIES FOR CONTINUING EDUCATION

Economic security, intelligently and constructively used, offers enormous opportunities for achieving "the good life." But plans for attaining intelligent use of leisure and the development of lifelong service and learning as an alternative to work must be based on sound principles. Several contributors to *The Guaranteed Income,* edited by Robert Theobald, provide us with relevant insights around which alternatives can be developed.

Marshall McLuhan, Eric Fromm, and Conrad Arensberg suggest slightly different but basically similar analyses of the elements necessary for social change. They all indicate that change is the product of past practices, values, content, and mores as well as new ideas and innovations. They also suggest that new concepts that do not take cognizance of the past and that do not build upon it are likely to fail.

More specifically, McLuhan cautions that we are inclined to look at new situations through preceding ones. He says, "Each new age creates an environment whose content is the preceding age. The content is perceptible. The environment is not." Applying McLuhan's analysis to the prospect of developing a satisfactory alternative to work and widespread acceptance of a life of learning it seems that our content today in education is primarily concerned with full public education from kindergarten through college. At the same time the environment—which we do not as yet perceive—is one in which we are really moving into an era in which education will be from C to G, or Cradle to Grave, rather than K to C.

Conrad Arensberg, discussing social change from the point of view of an anthropologist, suggests that there are three possible reactions to new challenges to society. "Ruin, revolution and evolution are always probabilities of today and alternatives for tomorrow." Discussing the possible reactions to a social challenge, Arensberg says, "The first effect of a successfully adaptive biological innovation of any kind is to hold on to something tried and true, to conserve the old in the face of change. The second effect of a successfully adaptive innovation of any kind, biological or social, is quite other than conservative; indeed it is the opening of a vast new door, a splendid serendipity." Arensberg's analysis, closely related to McLuhan's, again suggests the two components, of relationship to past experience and mores accompanied by innovation and invention.

Of direct relevance as to how the break from the old can be made and how the challenge and response of guaranteed income can be met through innovations in the field of continuing education is Arensberg's statement that "tribes, city-states, nations and civilizations before ours have all responded to new productive possibilities and faced new horizons for which they had to *organize and invent institutions* in order to realize the gains of their new powers." In the following section we will talk more about this need for inventing new institutions to realize the gains of our new powers.

Concerning the possibility of achieving adaptive social change in the face of cybernation, Eric Fromm discusses the question of whether Basic Economic Security will reduce the incentive for work and proceeds to analyze commonly held values in human beings. He suggests that, "A psychology of scarcity produces anxiety, envy and egotism" whereas, "A psychology of abundance produces initiative, faith in life, solidarity." He goes on to say, "I believe, . . . that it can be demonstrated that material incentive is by no means the only incentive for work and effort. First of all there are other incentives: pride, social recognition, pleasure in work (or learning or study) itself, etc." Fromm then goes on to point out that concepts such as honor, loyalty, and duty were motivating factors in earlier societies; that man by nature is not lazy; and that, "misuse of the guaranteed income would disappear after a short time, just as people would not overeat sweets after a few weeks, assuming that they would not have to pay for them." Fromm also appears to believe, based both on current psychology and former civilizations, that it is possible to insert other values and incentives to replace those of working for an income and for basic economic essentials.

Finally, A. H. Maslow, in his book *Motivation and Personality,* suggests that human needs are arranged hierarchically, from the lowest and most fundamental to the highest, and that a higher need is not activated until a person has attained some level of satisfaction of the needs below it. Maslow's suggested hierarchy from the most fundamental need to the highest is survival, safety, belonging, recognition, achievement, self-realization. Let us apply this formulation to the question under discussion—whether it is possible to develop values in our society that will make lifelong learning and recreational or educational achievement as acceptable as economic success. It would appear that as the lower and more basic needs are met, people may indeed seek and find satisfaction of other needs such as recognition, achievement, and self-realization—all of which could be fulfilled as much through a life of learning and service as through one of economic striving and accomplishment.

Bringing together these brief summaries of some of the ideas and thinking of McLuhan, Arensberg, Fromm, and Maslow it is possible to suggest certain conditions that are necessary if we are to develop a society in which lifelong learning and social service can replace job and economic success as a way of life. These conditions are

(1.) The more basic human needs must be satisfied before man becomes aware of and activates the higher needs in the hierarchy. (Presumably as Basic Economic Security provides for the needs of survival and safety it becomes possible to build a system that is concerned with the higher needs.) Thus any program for replacing economic success with other goals must assure the fulfillment of the needs for belonging, recognition, achievement, and self-realization.

(2.) The new society should build upon incentives of pride, social recognition, and pleasure in work (or study, or learning, or service). Concomitantly, in a psychology of abundance it is possible to produce initiative, faith in life, and solidarity. Thus our program must aim at producing these qualities and must accent the incentives of social recognition and pride in work.

(3.) Since reactions to new challenges to society may result either in ruin, revolution, or evolution and since, according to both Arensberg and McLuhan, social change is brought about by a combination of old values, mores, and subject matter as well as new and adaptive and creative behavior, it is essential that a new program of lifelong learning and service must build upon past practices and values rather than departing or, attempting to depart, completely from them.

In the final section of this essay we will attempt to suggest a plan of action and program that will make it possible to move toward the hoped-for life of learning and service, which can be made possible through a system of Basic Economic Security.

A PLAN AND PROGRAM FOR LIFELONG LEARNING AND COMMUNITY SERVICE

The major question that confronts adult and continuing educators is whether they can meet the challenge of abundance, leisure, and economic security with new inventions or whether they will merely stand by and watch and thus the new affluence will become a lost educational opportunity. The following, we believe, are the essential ingredients of a responsive and creative plan for continuing education.

1. A national program of lifelong learning must be based on new kinds of goals, incentives, and rewards that will provide recognition just as much for learning and service as for economic success. This will make it possible to feel as great a sense of achievement for these purposes as for a paid job; and will make the path to full self-realization an accepted and prized way of life rather than an offbeat and deviant kind of behavior. In other words our values and rewards must be expanded so that the desired life of learning will become accepted and prized by all.

How can this be done? Our task as educators is to plan actively to gain acceptance, visibility, and recognition for these changing values. It should not be too difficult to convince the leaders in the country of the value of initiative, faith in life, and solidarity. These are not new values and they meet the conditions established by Arensberg and McLuhan for building on the past. The value of Grecian "happiness" also is not new or different but rather is part of the basic warp and woof of our Judeo-Christian culture. The problem, therefore, is one of gaining general visibility for such values and for providing greater rewards for persons who live by them. To do this we must develop a multifaceted program that becomes an essential ingredient of our education from the beginning and that is reflected continually in our mass media and communications channels. In the early years of education we will need new folk heroes: Einsteins, T. S. Eliots, Deweys, Picassos, Helen Hayeses, and Nobel prizewinners rather than the generals and tycoons who star in history books as the "real" heroes of the United States. We must convince the mass media to esteem, discuss, expose to the public and acclaim the men of the mind and the legions who serve humanity for altruistic reasons. If it is now possible for the mass media to popularize mouthwashes, detergents, violence, and tawdriness it should also be possible for them to popularize, support, and develop values more consistent with a life of economic security. And in doing so we must utilize the new concepts and opportunities of our "electronic revolution" described by McLuhan.

Along with this enlistment of the mass media in a total and continuing campaign to develop and gain acceptance for our new values we must develop some system of rewards for achievement in education and service. Self-realization, the pinnacle of the needs, will provide a reward in itself. We will, however, need some kind of new academies in all of our communities, membership in which will be restricted to persons who attain a certain level of independent study and learning and in which dialogue and discourse become the meat of the academies. And these should not be restricted to a few outstanding thinkers but should be geared to the searchers and the learners as well as to the professors. There must also be some prized reward for those who make exceptional and continuing contributions in the field of voluntary service. It is premature to suggest the exact nature of such recognition at this time but there is a need to establish a national commission that will develop appropriate rewards as well as enlist the aid of the mass media in inculcating new values.

2. The special problem of involving the undereducated, the underprivileged, and the alienated members of our society in the hoped-for life of learning and service must be addressed directly and imaginatively. New kinds of educational methods, materials, curricula, and programs must be developed for the alienated portion of our population. They must be built upon a sound understanding of the needs and aspirations of this group and must aim to fulfill the hierarchy of needs in a planned and progressive manner.

These disadvantaged members of our society are our first large group of technologically unemployed, because they are becoming unemployable as machines and computers already developed take over their jobs. Since there are still labor shortages in many fields, our present efforts to deal with the situation are concentrated in basic education and vocational training. The intention is to make the labor supply fit the needs of the job market. These efforts are also linked with the value placed on work in our society, and our strong feeling that no person can be self-respecting if he is not gainfully employed and able to take responsibility for himself and his family.

While labor shortages persist and these attitudes prevail, it is unlikely that continuing education for the unemployed will change much; vocational efforts will continue to be the mode. More is being heard, however, about upgrading, and many of the vocational programs now offered have as their objective the acquisition of skills that are better paid and have a somewhat greater chance of survival into the age of cybernation.

The disadvantage to be overcome by continuing education with this group is that their impoverished lives have prevented them from developing the interests and attitudes that would enable them to deal constructively with a life of leisure. Furthermore, their school experience has often been so bad that they do not believe education can help them in any way. The economic barrier also keeps many from participating in adult education activities, since most programs cost money. Adult education has traditionally been required to be self-supporting in a way that neither secondary nor higher education has ever had to be.

Considering the magnitude of these inhibiting factors, it is easy to see why continuing education faces an enormous challenge in its efforts to work with the unemployed and now unemployable in the society. And even if BES becomes a reality during the next few years, it still would not be adequate to provide this group with sufficient resources to finance its own educational needs.

Obviously there are no easy paths toward success in involving poor people in continuing education. One promising portent, however, is the growth of a wide variety of action programs in disadvantaged communities. Continuing education can assist indigenous groups in developing the organizational and leadership skills necessary if they are to achieve more control over their communities and their lives. It can also help them in building up and rehabilitating their neighborhoods.

We must salvage and enormously enlarge activities such as those initiated by the Office of Economic Opportunity Community Action Programs, and we must be willing to utilize the successful organizational techniques espoused by Saul Alinsky to satisfy the need for "belonging." By starting at this point it would be possible to introduce a variety of educational programs related to local organizations, which would also help in providing "recognition" in the community. Alternatives to recognition for antisocial behavior are also essential, and these can probably best be provided through indigenous and aggressive community action organizations. Once the needs for "belonging" and "recognition" have been met it should be possible to merge the interests and desires of these no-longer-alienated people into the rest of society and to have them share in the other kinds of continuing education programs that lead to a sense of achievement and "self-realization."

What is required is a commitment to the goal of raising these disadvantaged people and communities to a decent level of living and to achieve this goal the necessary resources must be made available. The vast power of our intellectual potential and technological skill must be used as needed for planning and carrying out programs that will advance the level of living and the personal satisfaction of this too-long neglected segment of our society.

3. Basic changes and amendments must be made in our total elementary, secondary, and higher education systems that will inculcate the desire and the skills for lifelong learning in our future adults. Childhood curiosity, enthusiasm for ex-

ploration and discovery, and a sense of wonder—which at the outset know no socioeconomic boundaries—are often stamped out by the time a child gets through elementary school. It is rarely rekindled during secondary school and college. There are, fortunately, some exceptions at all levels to prove that education need not inhibit curiosity and originality. But these exceptions are not sufficiently widespread to have any marked impact on society. As a result, graduates at each educational level feel that they "have had it" educationally, that they are already educated sufficiently and therefore their enthusiasm for continuing education and independent study is effectively drowned.

If we are to make the most of guaranteed security, affluence, and leisure we must develop persons who will fully expect their education to be lifelong. To make this possible our educational institutions must modify their approach so as to instill in the student a desire for lifelong learning and provide him with the skills for independent study and inquiry. Existing curricula will have to be revised and the element of continuity will have to be built into educational programs from preschool to graduate school; courses must be taught not for static information and choice but rather to stimulate curiosity, to focus on important and significant topics, and to end with evaluation focused on the development of the capacity to ask intelligent questions and to plan for continuing the inquiry that was begun at school. In addition, schools at all levels must include courses that will teach the skills required in self-study, research, and inquiry so as to equip future adults to use traditional sources of information as well as the newly developing systems for information storage and retrieval.

4. Institutions of higher education, especially, must reorient their goals and programs to meet the needs for lifelong learning in an affluent and secure society. They must also broaden their scope and commitment to include responsibility for the continuing education of their graduates through special programs for managers and workers on sabbaticals, by

bringing doctors, lawyers, and engineers up to date on new developments in their fields, through a revamping of alumni associations so that they become the audience for continuing education as well as athletic activities and through a vastly expanded system of education for leisure for those sufficiently educated to participate in university-level programs. The urban public universities must develop new concepts of urban extension and community problem-solving so that their research and teaching resources are focused on the immediate problems of urban life.[2]

5. New kinds of institutional forms, organizational arrangements, and supporting services must be developed to provide for relevant, accessible, and comprehensive programs of continuing education at the community level. At the moment, almost all adult and continuing education programs and activities are outgrowths, offshoots, or minor modifications of programs initially developed for younger persons or adjuncts to programs in which continuing education is a secondary purpose. The buildings, the teachers, the programs, and the materials ordinarily utilized for continuing education were developed for youth and by and large have been merely slightly modified in adult education.

There is a great need for a new institutional form—a comprehensive "Uncommon School" or College in every major community—which is planned, developed, housed, operated, and staffed primarily for the purpose of adult and continuing education. Such new "Uncommon Schools" must provide effective counseling and tutorial service to assist adults to embark on their own independent programs of study. They must include new learning and knowledge centers that make available to adults studying either independently or in groups new systems for information storage and retrieval for all kinds of

[2] For a more complete discussion and series of recommendations concerning the role of universities in a comprehensive program of continuing education in the future, see A. A. Liveright, "The Uncommon College," in *Campus 1980,* New York: Dial Press, 1967.

audio as well as visual educational resources. This new "Uncommon School" must also provide residential facilities so that adult students may live in them extended periods of time while they are involved in educational programs. In addition to a central city campus, there should also be adjunct campuses in other locations in the city as well as in the suburbs. To permit adults to have a realistic way of checking their educational development we will also need a nationwide system of evaluation (which can be self-administered) so that learners will be able to measure progress toward their self-selected goals. It would also enable tutors to help them to assess their educational needs.

This new institutional form—the "Uncommon School"—should serve as the hub not only for independent liberal education and studies but also should be the focus in the community for health, family development, recreation, and self-fulfillment programs. It should bring together the many resources already existing for continuing education with the growing needs and interests that will develop in an increasingly affluent society. The "Uncommon School" should also concern itself with education for public and civic responsibility and should cooperate with colleges and universities, the government, and especially the mass media in producing and developing new kinds of public affairs programs that provide not only for "moving information," in McLuhan's terms, but also for two-way communication and feedback. Although it is not possible to point to any one prototype for this "Uncommon School" of the future it is possible to suggest some institutions in some communities in the United States that already encompass at least one of the elements mentioned above.

6. A totally new kind of curriculum and organization of learning experiences must be developed to provide for a meaningful, flexible, and challenging program of lifelong learning. As Robert Blakely said in *The Homeodynamic Society* we must have a situation "where everyone is learning

from everyone all the time." In the first place the total structure for securing credit and degrees must be modified so that adults can work toward a degree primarily through tutorials and independent study. They must also be given credit through examinations for learning gained outside of school; and they must be able to move toward a degree at a pace appropriate to adults who have other responsibilities. (Steps in this direction have already been taken through the various college special degree programs now in operation, through provisions for advanced standing, and through the Council On College Level Examinations.) Through effective community counseling services, adults must be permitted to participate in educational programs at all levels along with the regular full-time younger students. The inclusion of older men and women in these programs will not only raise the level of discussion and provide an added element of mature experience but will also serve as living proof to the young that continuing education is indeed a way of life. As far as non-credit informal continuing education is concerned, the new "Uncommon Schools"—or centers for continuing education—will develop curricula free from the limits of traditional subject-matter fields. Their educational program will be planned around adult life-roles. Programs will be established in the areas of (1) professional and vocational competence (for those who are still employed and who wish to keep up to date in their fields); (2) family and personal competence (to include learning related to family, health, psychological, intergroup, and welfare problems); (3) civic and social competence (related to education for public responsibility, political effectiveness, local, state, national, and international affairs); and (4) education for self-realization (including primarily programs in liberal education and intellectual development). The "Uncommon School" will not only rely on the best teachers from schools, colleges, and universities who enjoy discussions and dialogues with mature adults, they will also make maximum use of key professionals employed by industry and the government as adjunct faculty. They will also draw on the continually growing reservoir of persons outside of the labor market whose areas of special knowledge are identified in the central learning center and who have had special preparation as teachers of adults. In addition, the rapidly growing need for counselors and tutors for lifelong learning will be filled largely by persons who themselves are enrolled as learners and who will switch back and forth from a student to a tutorial or counseling role. The curriculum, the "teacher-learners," the methods, the locale, and indeed the content will always be subject to modification by planning and curriculum committees, which will operate in each of the four divisions of the "Uncommon School." A Utopian dream? Possibly, but in fact a school developed somewhat along these lines did operate for a number of years in San Francisco under the leadership of Alexander Miekeljohn. In those days it was an idea before its time, but there is no reason why this challenging concept should not be revived now that its time has come.

7. To provide another outlet for the interest and energies of adults who are no longer involved in jobs, work, or the regular labor market there must be a great expansion and better organization of the already vast field of volunteer service. Millions of Americans are active and involved in some kind of volunteer service ranging from "Candy-Stripers," Big Brothers, hospital aides, money-raisers for non-profit organizations, to members of service corps, tutors, and consultants to various kinds of organizations.

It is suggested that a career in community, national, and international service on a volunteer basis is already a rewarding activity for persons no longer in the labor market. It can become an even more significant way of utilizing the energy and interests and of satisfying the needs for belonging, recognition, achievement, and self-realization of vastly increased numbers of adults in the future. To move such service to a status that is nationally recognized and adequately rewarded will require a greater degree of professionalization and wider acceptance of service as a significant activity in our society. We need better information about the voluntary opportunities that already exist—as a starting point. We need to develop new kinds of volunteer tasks and positions. We need to develop career lines whereby volunteers can move from the simpler and less demanding tasks to more complicated and responsible positions. We need professional training, which is required for participation in volunteer work at all levels, and, finally, we need some kind of significant national recognition for volunteer service. It is possible that as leisure, affluence and Basic Economic Security become realities we should move toward a federal cabinet level Department of Volunteer Service.

8. To translate the preliminary ideas developed in this chapter, and in others in this book, effective research is required about the human problems that will develop in a non-work oriented society. Although there is now some research in this area it is pitifully sparse and ridiculously underfinanced when compared to R and D funds available for weapons, space exploration, and supersonic transport. Large-scale additional psychological, anthropological, and sociological research is required to produce effective solutions to the problems of involving the underprivileged and those who have never worked in a learning society. Additional research is required into means for changing value systems and existing value orientations and for overcoming cultural lags in our society. We also need vastly increased research and experimentation into the more effective use of the new technology for learning and education and into the ways in which communication techniques and practices can be utilized for socially desirable learning rather than for commercially oriented or politically motivated thought-control. Research for leisure and security is required if we are to develop the kind of education that will enable our citizens to make the best use of their new leisure.

9. To foster the kind of research and experimentation outlined in this chapter there is a need for a national organization to coordinate and study problems, needs, and programs in continuing education in a free and affluent society. No mechanism now exists for communication between the investigations now in progress. Interdisciplinary approaches have not been adequately developed and no effective overall efforts are now being made to plan long-term programs nor to secure support for such research and planning.

In view of the extent to which industry is responsible for rapid advances in cybernation and for the impact of these developments on society and because the problems that will develop will require national action, there is strong logic in proposing that the funds for needed research and development should be financed jointly by private industry and the federal government.

The promise of the future in a society free from toil and want is the freedom for every individual to achieve his best self, his highest creativity, his most satisfying service, and his most considered responsibility. It is indeed the "exercise of vital powers along the lines of excellence," that has been the vision of dreamers in every age.

It is a promise within our grasp. But we must marshal our genius and our resources now to make it come to fulfillment in orderly and reasoned steps, otherwise we must expect domination by the machines we created to be our servants.

MANDATE FOR LEARNING

Don Benson

Thump, thump, thump! Rabbits signal to one another today much as they have for thousands of years. Within a few miles of my home in Vermont, I can find varieties of furry creatures (including rabbits), birds, bugs, fish, and plants that relate to one another and their respective environments much as they did when the human population of this planet numbered less than one hundred million.

But the manner in which people relate to one another, and their respective environments, has changed drastically—even in Vermont. Moreover, according to current accounts of man's technical progress, the rate of change has increased markedly. Technical advances of vast consequences for the patterning of human society, and for the relationship of human society to this region of Universe, are now occurring yearly. Fresh thinking and fresh social forms are also emerging with startling rapidity.

Of course there are new expressions. Reality has been integrated into the electronic era, and young persons are "turning on." This new reality generates important questions such as, "Am I tuned in?" And disturbing questions such as "Am I plugged in?"

In order to be plugged in and stay plugged in, a person needs to know what's happening in the real world. This essay represents my attempt to grasp what's happening to education. Specifically, what will happen to education if people are economically secure. I hope, hereby, to ward off obsolescence (to be and stay plugged in a little longer) both for myself and for whoever ponders these words.

We are living in a period of transition between an age of

mechanical technology and an age of electronic technology. In terms of human relations, I would suggest that this transition can be accurately described as progression from an "age of earning" to an "age of learning." The idea is that automation will eliminate most of the jobs people have been required to do in order to earn a living, and people (you and me, for example) will have to function on higher levels. Since we shall not be able to function on these higher levels unless we are economically secure, we shall find some way of guaranteeing ourselves adequate incomes. Once we have unconditional incomes on at least subsistence levels, then it will no longer be suitable to talk of earning a living—for we shall be faced with a new sort of problem, that of learning a living. (Many people have already had to face this problem.)

1. THE AGE OF EARNING

MECHANICAL TECHNOLOGY FRAGMENTS LIFE

Man has always been confronted with the problem of survival. Our success in not only maintaining but increasing the human population of earth has resulted (in part) from breaking the problem down into more manageable proportions—how to get food, how to get from here to there, how to keep warm, how to make decisions, and so on. By facing problems in an ever more precise manner, we have greatly extended our capacity to survive. The development of specialized functions (as meat inspector, train switcher, lathe operator, etc.) and the disciplining of people reliably to perform specialized functions has thus been a very important type of technological advance.

In order to take advantage of mechanical technology, it is essential to have people adjust to fragmented and repetitive routines. Workers are needed to run machines that perform single, separate operations. Workers are needed to move things about. Efficiency is achieved by reducing difficult operations to simple sequences and performing them repeatedly. Integration of the many specialized functions that are performed within the productive and distributive facilities of society is achieved through standardization of products and uniformity of procedures.

BUREAUCRACY INTEGRATES THE FRAGMENTS

The organizational form that coordinates socioeconomic activity during the mechanical age is structured along the lines of a pyramid. At the lowest level, in a factory, individual workers are held responsible for operating individual machines. Foremen are held responsible for the production of groups of men and machines. White-collar workers are held responsible for shuffling paper in such a way as to maintain the integration of what is below them. Outside of factories, people are held responsible for maintaining the link between producers and consumers. At the highest levels are individuals who coordinate vast resources and needs. The leaders and bosses are presumed to control all operations performed under them in the pyramid.

With the advent of literacy, it became possible to have detailed laws and beliefs that applied to great numbers of people. It became possible to exercise authority in a more comprehensive way than ever before. The advent of mass literacy meant that great numbers of people living in a contiguous land area could share a common literature and regard themselves as a unit—a nation-state. This gave people a great sense of power: the thought that they did not stand alone but participated in the glory of an entire nation. Those who read Christian literature participated in the glory of Christendom. Classicists participated in the glory of civilization. Readers of American literature participated in the glory of America. Readers of Communist literature participated in the glory of communism. Suddenly, whole generations were on the make, building grand and glorious empires in the wilderness of the world. Thus began a progressive series of initiatives, innovations, and inventions that led to the mechanical age.

Persons living in the mechanical age know that new ideas come to nothing until there is an army behind them. In order for a few men to have their dreams come true, they must devote their entire lives (plus the lives of hundreds of other men) to the task. For every mechanical dream-come-true, a hundred men must spend their lives in specialized and repetitive toil. Patriotic ideas require armies of patriots. Inventions require industrial armies. Religious ideas depend upon armies of church-goers.

PEOPLE ARE MADE TO CONFORM THROUGH POSITIVE AND NEGATIVE SANCTIONS

But man has distinguished himself in an evolutionary sense by rejecting the stable governments that ants find so useful and by avoiding the dead ends that species run into when they become specialized and unresponsive to general changes in their environment. Men do not take easily to specialization, and, when they do concentrate on one thing for a while, they become eager for new and different experiences. What this means is that men must be bribed, coerced, manipulated, regimented, and duped in order to fit into any kind of mechanical routine. How, then, have some men been able to build empires?

They have built empires by harnessing fellowmen as mules, offering carrots to those who move in the assigned direction and firmly kicking the rumps of those who balk. Hunger, the desire for decent shelter and medical care, and the hope to keep a wife are rather rudimentary motives. People who hold power in the mechanical age—no matter how much or how little, whether in terms of money, the authority to give credit, or the right to vote—speak to these motives, saying, "If you do thus and so, you will be fed and mated . . . and comfortable by and by." Whereupon men generally do thus and so. Historically there has never been enough for everybody, and there have always been plenty of people whose condition is clearly wretched, so reasonable men do what is required—to put things between themselves and the lower depths.

A brief examination of religion, psychology, and education reveals how people can be induced to conform to mechanical patterns. Persons primarily concerned with religion in the mechanical age must earn their daily bread by establishing financial relations with a sizable group. On the one hand, the clergy must indoctrinate the laity in such a way that they will offer up their money. On the other hand, the clergy must not deviate from patterns the laity will support. The result is rigidly organized, church-centered religion. The churches offer comfort to those who are not fulfilled in the mechanical order by proclaiming that there is a higher authority in whom one can find justice, love, and eternal life. Very comforting to the man who has a tyrant for a boss, but it's a little hard on the individual who prefers neither to have a boss nor to be one.

Mechanical-age psychology pounces on "abnormality." The main purpose of this psychology is to classify people and find out what makes them "tick," so that authorities may know just how to fit them into the existing order. In many cases, authorities have to lock people up. But most people can be conditioned to respond to a wide range of positive and negative sanctions (as rats in mazes) in such a way that they will be normal and well adjusted.[1]

Education is conducted according to the standard bureaucratic model. Usually, one person is given primary responsibility for the allocation of all finances within a given school system. In order to discharge this responsibility, he must know, or be able to find out, what everyone and anyone in the

[1] A general text reflecting the psychology of classification and adjustment is Floyd L. Ruch, *Psychology and Life*, Chicago: Scott, Foresman, 1953.

system is doing. If the system is quite large, he must establish all sorts of rules, regulations, and standard procedures. Good schools prepare people to do what they are told on rather high levels of competence and sophistication. They produce graduates much as factories produce finished products. But it is practically impossible in the mechanical age to run a school that allows for very much learning in the sense of being curious, making explorations, and developing personal intelligence.

EXTREME CONFORMITY DOES NOT ALLOW FOR LIFE

Large, centrally directed organizations, staffed with well adjusted personnel, spring up everywhere in the mechanical age because they work. They are also dangerous. They are dangerous because they can become big and clumsy like dinosaurs. Bureaucracies devour the creative energies of many, many people and walk heavily across the land. If any single centrally directed organization were allowed to exist without checks or balances and evolve to its logical end-point, it would eliminate all non-conformity to the extent of eliminating life. In the end, there would be peace, order, and stability: the entire world would be turned into a pyramid as a fitting monument to authority. It is doubtful, however, that pyramidal structures will ever evolve to the point of taking over the world.

COMPETITION IS A SAFEGUARD AGAINST EXTREME CONFORMITY

Fortunately for Americans, the American socioeconomy has traditionally included a repertoire of checks and balances, which have tended to restrain pyramid builders. The main thing is competition. Organizations that become too rigid are left by the wayside as more dynamic and responsive organizations come into being. Politicians are voted out of office. Business firms lose money to their competitors. On a global scale, nations maintain their vitality by competing with one another. The Soviet Union has made substantial progress, despite limitations on internal competition, largely because it is competing with the United States.

NEW WEAPONS THREATEN TO ELIMINATE COMPETITION

Unfortunately, competition can get out of hand. The original purpose of laissez-faire capitalism as set forth by Adam Smith was to free people so they could be creative. But sometimes it is not the most creative person or organization that emerges. It is the person or organization that has the greatest power to cripple or destroy the competitor.[2] When there is a secure authority who can effectively limit competition to the creative sphere, then competition can be highly creative. Today, however, there is not even the possibility of having an authority who can limit competition to the creative sphere. How could an authority prevent electronic eavesdropping, for example? Imagine even a strong world authority trying to prevent destruction in a time when a few "value-free" scientists can mess up the planet for everybody.

Competition depends upon the continued existence of competitors. It breaks down when competitors can cripple or annihilate one another. On the other hand, if the competitors are in close enough communication with one another (as competitors will increasingly be with the aid of electronic information nets), they cease to be competitiors because they can no longer be considered as independent entities.

[2] Cf. "Big Corporations Can Have Their Own CIA," *The New Republic*, February 18, 1967, p. 18.

2. THE TRANSITION

ELECTRONIC TECHNOLOGY REINTEGRATES LIFE

The mechanical operations that used to be separate are now being cybernetically linked by electronic computers. Men are less and less needed for specialized, repetitive toil. Moreover, men's minds are ceasing to be dominated by positive and negative sanctions from local authorities. Through a plethora of communications channels, men are inundated with immediate information from their total environment. Information is beginning to flow around earth just as rapidly as information flows around a jelly fish, a chipmunk, or a human person.

There appears to be a standard transmission time for information moving between points in an organism. If the points are very close (as points within the same cellular neighborhood) the velocity of transmission is less than one meter per second. For longer distances such as we find in a giant squid or a two-meter man, the transmission rate is on the order of one hundred meters per second. For a viable world society, then, the transmission rate would have to be on the order of one hundred thousand kilometers per second to compensate for global distances. With information traveling at the speed of light via Telstar, we now have a technological basis for reintegrating the lives of individual human beings and newly integrating the lives of all human beings.

BUREAUCRACY IS NO LONGER FUNCTIONAL

Pyramidal structures work best when there are routine jobs to be done. But routine jobs are being automated. There is such a rate of change and growth in level of complexity and degree of interrelation in all of man's activities today that bureaucracies simply cannot cope. Leaders can scarcely comprehend the work that now needs to be done, much less direct it.

Positive and negative sanctions cease to be adequate. When a group of men can produce enough to live on only if they toil steadily, it makes sense to say, "Those who do not work may not eat." In a complex society such as ours, however, the need is for love, imagination, and concern for the relationship of man as a total human being with his total environment. What will happen to discipline when people discover that individuals wandering in the woods may be doing more productive work than individuals slaving behind desks? Perhaps the authorities will maintain discipline in the following manner: "Be loving or we'll lock you up." "Solve one of man's pressing problems, and we'll give you a merit badge plus fifty thousand dollars and a vacation in the Bahamas."

Current operations are too big and complex to be controlled in the old sense. Now it is necessary to have shared purposes to which people can relate on a cooperative basis. In the mechanical age, it is enough for a man to want to feed his kids. The boss can tell him, "Do this, and your kids will be fed." He can do the job and worry about his kids at the same time. Only part of his personality is required. But to solve the problems of landing astronauts on the moon it is necessary to have men who want to land astronauts on the moon and would spend all their time thinking about it even at subsistence wages.

COMPETITION IS NO LONGER FUNCTIONAL

Indeed, the directors of American society have recognized the need for more cooperation, and they are cooperating very closely among themselves. What the directors are not doing is subjecting their operations, methods, and values to public scrutiny. Rather, they are gathering enormous quantities of information on the general population; they are developing highly sophisticated techniques for staying at the helm and preventing people from rocking the boat.[3]

PEOPLE ARE LOSING CONFIDENCE IN MECHANICAL FORMS

Meanwhile, people are beginning to entertain grave doubts about their leaders. There is a growing realization that scientists who do not struggle with and face the question of higher values are actually subject to lower values. Not only is scientific work increasingly governed by the insane priorities of huge power establishments, it is influenced by the unresolved psychological hang-ups of individual scientists.

People are beginning to suspect that the majority of existing institutions—schools, churches, cities, businesses, governmental bodies, etc.—no longer serve human beings, that human beings are being fed into these organizations just to keep them going. The general failure of mechanical forms is exemplified by the war in Vietnam. It appears that hundreds of thousands of young men are being sent to do a job in Vietnam because there isn't enough unpleasant work at home to serve as a basis for keeping them in the job system. (If young men are allowed to get started doing what they want to do, the whole U.S. power structure will be put out of business.) The war in Vietnam is so gross and so brutal that the American people may not be able to stomach it—or the pyramid builders whose purposes it serves—much longer.

LSD has become very popular because it enables people to withdraw their creative energies from the system. It enables a young person to stop supporting the awful dinosaur,

[3] Cf. Andrew Kopkind, "The Future Planners," *The New Republic*, February 25, 1967, and Max Ways, "The Road to 1977," *Fortune*, January 1967.

and it becomes a way of life while he is looking around for something better to do.

There is a growing number of people—acid-heads, scientists, artists, clergymen, regular people with decency and good sense—who are really groping for values and for worthwhile communities. They are convinced we need a radically new world order and would gladly give their lives to bring it about if only they had a little better idea of what the new order could be and how to achieve it.

RESPECT FOR AUTHORITY IS NO LONGER FUNCTIONAL

These seekers of human values do not want to be told anything: they feel their direction must come from within. It has been the function of authority to tell people what to do and what not to do. Machine systems now do what authority wants done, and people are left with the orders about what not to do. They know that taking directions from external sources will result only in frustration. Order in human affairs now depends upon common purposes rather than recognized authority. It is recognized that authority is dead. In place of authority, people are now prepared to recognize beautiful aspirations in their fellowmen.[4]

A NEW VISION OF MAN IS APPEARING AGAINST THE BACKDROP OF UNIVERSE

A sense of man's common purposes and his role in the events of Universe is emerging with sufficient clarity that it can be expressed in rather precise terms. Since this sense of purpose is emerging out of man's experience with electronic technology, it will reach and involve those who use electronic

[4] Cf. Erich Fromm, *You Shall Be as Gods,* New York: Holt, 1966.

technology just as surely as the idea of authority takes hold of those who lives are structured by mechanical technology.

By taking an overview of certain general observations made by numerous scientists, it is possible to conclude that there are two basic functions occurring in Universe. On the one hand, we have the observation of astronomers, based on spectroscopic analysis of light from distant stellar sources, that Universe is expanding. The expanding Universe observation is in accord with the law of entropy, which refers to energy dissipation, as in combustion. Entropy is described by mathematicians as an increase of random elements. When a bomb explodes, it results in an increase of random elements, which take up more space than the bomb. Thus one of the functions occurring in Universe is an explosive function involving expansion and disorganization.

On the other hand, we may assume from the principle of complementarity, advanced by the physicist Niels Bohr, that if there is an explosive function in Universe there must also be an implosive function involving contraction and organization, i.e. a synergetic function resulting in a decrease of random elements. Indeed, we can find many examples of this function. At various time/places, some of the hydrogen and helium that is said to comprise about 99 per cent of Universe contracts into a swirling mass and forms a star. Now, on the surface, a mature star such as our sun may appear to function entropically, in the sense that it radiates energy out into space, but inside the sun something else occurs: hydrogen, under intense heat and pressure, is converted into heavier elements. These heavier elements, such as carbon, oxygen, and nitrogen, are eventually spewed out into space where they can accumulate, form into molecules, and condense into planets. Stars, then, are partially synergetic in that they organize galactic material into higher forms.[5]

[5] Here I am drawing on George Wald, "The Search for Common Ground," *Zygon: Journal of Religion and Science*, 1:1, University of Chicago Press, March 1966.

Planets seem to function primarily as concentrating centers. Our planet earth receives considerably more energy (in the form of solar radiation, star dust, cosmic rays, etc.) than it gives off. On our planet, much of the incoming energy is absorbed by plants and animals. Solar energy is used as fuel for the development and maintenance of a whole complex regenerative system of evolving life. Viruses in the presence of a suitable nutritive medium lay down their complex molecular structure in the medium, thus reproducing themselves. Plants draw on simple ingredients from the soil and grow in splendid profusion. Animals, operating in a mutually beneficial relation with plants, sort out the miscellaneous resources in their surroundings and rearrange them into complex systems highly organized in regenerative fashion, i.e. animals. Bertrand Russell has referred to this process as the "chemical imperialism of living matter."[6]

A number of frontier thinkers have concluded from observations of this sort that man's common purposes involve drawing together random elements and organizing them into orderly functional relationships: to maintain the expansion-contraction balance of Universe.[7] We may not have been conscious of our function during the mechanical age, but we have been performing it nonetheless. To an observer on Mars, this would be obvious. To some being on Mars who has closely observed the surface of earth during the last few thousand revolutions about the sun, the most striking development, overshadowing all others, would be the increase of the human population and the complex systems for the support of human life: agriculture, industry, transportation, social structures, cities, and towns. Some people may regard "chemical imperialism" as a thoroughly repulsive notion, but the observation remains: the net thrust of all human efforts up to now

[6] Bertrand Russell, *An Outline of Philosophy*, (Cleveland: Meridian Books, 1960), pp. 30–31.
[7] Cf. R. Buckminster Fuller, "Vision 65 Summary Lecture," *The American Scholar*, 35:2, Spring 1966.

has been to turn as much as possible of the matter/energy of earth into human beings.

If we arrange the humanly observed synergetic systems into a hierarchy of increasing ability to form order out of chaos, we find that human beings are the most synergetic systems of all. We have performed our function in many ways: as hunters, farmers, laborers, engineers, scientists, artists, and religious visionaries; as people who eat, sleep, exercise, think, and love one another.

This scientific-religious vision of man as a synergetic being is well grounded in twentieth-century thinking. It is now generally accepted that man has evolved from less highly organized forms of life. Many people would even argue that man has progressed. In the writings of Henri Bergson, Carl Jung, Teilhard de Chardin, and many others, the idea of life force or synergy is central. A growing number of psychologists (led by Abraham Maslow, current president of the American Psychological Association) have set aside their old concern with adjustment, and they have begun to take up the problem of human emergence.[8] A new journal has been started specifically to encourage the scientific-religious vision of man.[9]

The whole science of cybernetics is concerned with synergetic phenomena, which is to say "self-organizing systems." In cybernetic parlance, a "system" consists of entities in dynamic relationship with one another. A system is said to be "open" if entities outside the system influence components of the system (which influence is sometimes called "input") or if the components influence entities outside of the system (which influence is sometimes called "output"). Cyberneticists tend to concentrate on the internal processes of systems, as though they were dealing with "closed" systems, but the only true closed system (which is not subject to external in-

---

[8] A. H. Maslow, *Toward a Psychology of Being*, Princeton, N.J.: Van Nostrand, 1962.

[9] *Zygon: Journal of Religion and Science.*

fluences) is Universe. All of the various sub-systems are more or less open. If the input of a sub-system is more highly ordered than the output, we may say that the system functions entropically. If, on the other hand, the sub-system results in an increase of order, then we may describe it as a synergetic or self-organizing system.[10]

One of the truly remarkable results of the evolution of self-organizing systems has been the cooperation of human individuals in generating further systems that exhibit certain limited types of self-organizing behavior. Our computer-guided machine systems are in this class. But computer-guided machine systems are properly regarded as extensions of man,[11] performing sub-functions derived from the ongoing purpose of man—to implode and organize Universe. The fact that some men are currently in the position of competing with automatic machinery is merely due to an outmoded socioeconomic system that treats some men as automatic machinery and other men as programmers.

It will certainly be ironic if man fails during this period when he is becoming fully aware of his purpose for the first time. And there are many ways in which we might fail. We might, for example, allow random elements (pollutants) to accumulate in the earth, air, and water to such an extent that the entire biosphere will degenerate with all higher animals and most plants dying off. We might get involved in bio-chemical warfare to such an extent that nothing higher than complex molecules would survive. We might fail so miserably at generating fresh socioeconomic forms that are adequate to the electronic age that we will demolish our planet in frustration and send crude little radioactive lumps of earth screaming out into a degenerating Universe.

Those who are experiencing the new vision of man generally

[10] Consider earth: it has an input of solar energy and an output of astronauts.
[11] Cf. Marshall McLuhan, *Understanding Media: the Extensions of Man,* New York: McGraw-Hill, 1965.

believe (as many old apostles of free enterprise believe) that all hope for human survival on earth depends upon individuals functioning at ever-higher levels of self-organizing behavior. They believe (as existentialists believe) that when authorities "force" someone to do something they are merely limiting his range of choices. But the individual still chooses —between limiting his studies to assignments and thus satisfying his teachers or choosing to follow his interests and getting bad grades in school; between going into the Army and going to prison. What is needed socially is to increase the range of behavioral possibilities open to people. Long-haired boys are serving as shock troops in this movement. If the new visionaries are successful, then children will be allowed to learn and develop according to their individual organic priorities, much as students at Montessori schools have been allowed to do.[12] By supporting people in lifelong learning, so that individuals are always seeking to optimize their own unique behavioral patterns, it may be possible to provide a basis for organizational systems that can function efficiently despite the complexity, diversity, and rapid change that characterize our times.

3. THE AGE OF LEARNING

PYRAMIDAL STRUCTURES WILL BE SUPERSEDED BY ORGANIC-ADAPTIVE STRUCTURES[13]

We are all very familiar with top-down authority structures. And we may curse them: "Damn bureaucracy!" But curse the existing order as we may, there are very few people who

[12] Cf. Bernard Asbell, "Teach Thyself," *The New Improved American*, New York: Delta Books, 1966.
[13] The notation "organic-adaptive" comes from Warren G. Bennis, "The Coming Death of Bureaucracy," *Think*, November–December 1966.

can propose anything more realistic than Utopian communities in the hills for alternatives. Bureaucratic forms are evolving, however, and becoming so dynamic that they are ceasing to be bureaucratic. Anyone with a rough idea of the challenges currently facing the so-called Defense Department and the major corporations knows that these organizations would be in a complete state of chaos and degeneration if they were still functioning on strictly pyramidal lines. In fact, the degree of order that exists in the world today (outside of China) is largely due to the emergence of semi-autonomous purpose and problem-oriented groups, which are sometimes called "task forces." Order is maintained in Latin America by various U.S.-based task forces. Military dictatorships are totally incapable of maintaining order in the age of learning.

While tribal, monarchical, and bureaucratic forms of organization have precedents in monkey troups, beehives, and anthills, the organic-adaptive forms (exemplified by task forces) seem at first to be totally without precedent. The human central nervous system, however, provides a considerable range of precedents for these new social structures. In the lowest, most primitive regions of the human brain there are nerve cells or neurones, that function rather bureaucratically as they take care of routine processes such as digestion, circulation, breathing, etc. At higher levels, the neurones cooperate as task forces. Primitive areas of the brain take charge of simple tasks. Newer areas are responsible for complex tasks. In the frontal region, new brain, there are no predetermined purposes or functions at all, except for the general purpose of synergy.

One cannot examine the frontal region of the human brain and find some neurones that give orders while other neurones follow orders. If one neurone tried to tell the others what to do, they would stop listening to him until he learned a little more respect for their integrity. There is no pyramidal arrangement. Instead there is a kind of three-dimensional network in which each neurone maintains direct communication with about a dozen other neurones. Mass communication is a function of the primitive brain informing the body.[14] Communication is more personal and intelligent in the new brain. It involves dialogue in face-to-face communities. There is a participatory democracy[15] in which each neurone helps to define and implement objectives.

COMPETITION WILL BE SUPERSEDED BY DIALOGUE

Animals that possess only primitive brains cannot significantly modify their behavior. If the behavior is inadequate, they die. Men living in the age of earning do not voluntarily change their behavior and their ideas. If their behavior and their ideas are inadequate, they lose out in competition and they lose debates. But men of the electronic age are constantly learning. They are constantly modifying their behavior through interaction and their ideas through dialogue.

Our mechanical-age schools are obsolete. They are structured along the lines of automated factory-ism, and thus we can expect that task forces employing the new technology for educational purposes will simply move in and push aside our conventional school buildings, teachers, and administrators. Schoolmen may find this prospect disturbing. But let every teacher remember that he is first and foremost a person, and in his capacity as a person scarcely dreamed of new roles will open up for him.

[14] Cf. Thomas Hobbes, *Leviathan, or the Matter, Form, and Power of a Commonwealth, Ecclesiastical and Civil*, London, 1651. Also, G. M. Wyburn, R. W. Pickford, and R. J. Hirst, *Human Senses and Perception*, ed. G. M. Wyburn, University of Toronto Press, 1964.

[15] "Participatory democracy" is a slogan of Students for a Democratic Society.

RESOURCES WILL BE PROCESSED FROM EACH ACCORDING TO HIS NEED, TO EACH ACCORDING TO HIS ABILITY

The photographs and other information we receive from satellites make us increasingly aware of our total environment. People are developing great enthusiasm for Earth not as territory on which they can build empires, containing resources they can exploit, but as a living sphere they can develop as a never-ending work of art. With this awareness comes sadness; for the market system, which still coordinates the bulk of human activity and which works excellently on the level of producing and distributing better mousetraps, does not work very well on the level of coordinating artistic activity.

In relation to the new vision, the proper function of a socioeconomic system is to coordinate and support the synergetic functioning of man on earth. In a proper socioeconomic system, resources would be allocated from each according to his need (to function synergeticly), to each according to his ability (to function synergeticly). The idea is that persons, as self-organizing systems, naturally feel a need to be productive. We should take advantage of this. Persons also have various levels of ability to make productive use of various kinds and quantities of resources. If there is not enough food for everybody, then those who enjoy producing food should be encouraged, and they should be given those resources they can use efficiently in the production of food. If there is enough food, everybody should be given the food he can use to maintain or improve his health.

Application of this formula (whether on the level of food, clothing, shelter, or art) would not, of course, involve any central authority, dictating the input and the output of individuals. That would be absurd. In the age of learning, socioeconomic value judgments are decentralized; they are made by individuals engaged in dialogue.

THESE METHODS HAVE BEEN USED SUCCESSFULLY FOR
THOUSANDS OF YEARS

It would appear that the age of learning is a fantastic departure from all the previous ages of human experience. But a limited number of persons, those we have called geniuses, have been living in an age of learning all along. Consider Socrates, Aristotle, Christ, Michelangelo, Newton, the Founding Fathers, Freud, Einstein, Norbert Wiener, and so on. None of these men was tied into any pyramidal organization. All of these men were constantly engaged in dialogue, on some level. Each man had a community of dialogue in which to learn/live. There were the public places of Athens, Plato's Academy, the twelve Apostles, Florence, the Royal Society, conferences and letters, Vienna, and so on. Einstein developed his relativity theory at a time when he was accustomed to going for walks with friends, discussing ideas all night under the stars. In addition to corresponding with frontier thinkers around the world, Norbert Wiener belonged to an interdisciplinary supper club in Cambridge.

Further, it would be hard to name a genius who earned his living. Even those who held jobs, such as Einstein at the patent office, did not regard their income as pay for a job. They regarded their incomes as economic security that would enable them to go on living/learning. Picasso is what he does and does what he is. One can support him in his endeavors, but one cannot pay him.

Remind a schoolman that approximately all major advances in understanding are associated with persons who have rejected positive and negative sanctions, and he will say that geniuses are exceptions: most people won't learn anything unless you require them to. The point is that schools are not supposed to help persons develop real understanding or be creative. Schools don't even recognize persons as such.

The primary purpose of schooling is to transform human beings into personnel who will fit in and perform predetermined functions, but mainly fit in.

On the question of how to provide for the fullest development of human beings, relatively little work has been done. But we do know that it is helpful for people to have enough to eat and not be harassed too much. It is important to have rich sources of information and yet have opportunities for reflection, for activity that is not constantly interrupted by demands felt to be external. We know that, in societies where all members have to function fully in order to survive, the basic unit of organization is a small group including about a dozen adults.[16] We are discovering that significant learning does occur when diverse individuals voluntarily come together and really go to work with their entire personalities.[17] Approximately all major advances in the civil rights struggle can be traced back to depth encounters between individuals, meeting in small groups and engaging in dialogue.

Throughout history, men have been kept busy with required courses as it were, with a few exceptions. But there ceases to be any socioeconomic justification for continuing these requirements. Highly structured activity tends to be automated. The need today is for people to exercise their personal intelligence and to engage in dialogue about values. At the same time, there are a number of developments in electronic technology that are not only facilitating dialogue, they are making it practically impossible to avoid.

Consider electronic eavesdropping, for example. It's sure to increase. And what can we do about it? A person doing things he can't afford to have others know about has good reason to be paranoid. My own approach would be to follow

[16] Bushmen in the Kalahari Desert, for example.
[17] There have been remarkable successes in everything from transcending dope addiction to solving difficult technical problems in such focuses of dialogue as Synanon, the National Training Laboratories, Esalen Institute and Synectics, Inc.

my conscience in all things and seek to open channels of dialogue with the FBI agent or whoever happens to be investigating me. People may not soon learn to love those with whom they disagree, but they may learn to engage in dialogue with them, for their own protection. People will become so familiar with one another through bugging and counter-bugging they may as well be friends.

The development of inexpensive miniature communications transceivers will enable everyone to have his own electronic communications network. IT&T could provide such equipment to everyone in the world within two years. And if IT&T doesn't, some Japanese firm probably will. Within a decade, the entire population of the earth may be linked in a communications network quite similar to what is found in the human forebrain. This is analogous to what Chardin meant by "Noosphere."[18]

The growth of "Operation Match" type programs will significantly increase our sense of compatible purposes. First the computers were used to help lonely-hearts find mates. Then computers were used to facilitate dating among college students. Management consultant Dale Learn extended Operation Match to the level of matching men and jobs. Western Union has a program called "Personnel Information Communications System." The latest development involves extending Operation Match techniques into the area of dialogue education, enabling persons concerned with similar problems to get in touch with one another.[19] This idea of persons

---

[18] Teilhard de Chardin, *The Phenomenon of Man,* New York: Harper & Row, 1961. According to Don R. Swanson ("On Improving Communications Among Scientists," *Bulletin of the Atomic Scientists,* February 1966), many scientists have been dealing with the problem of information overload by exchanging information on a personal basis through networks of small groups called "invisible colleges." These invisible colleges constitute a kind of embrionic Noosphere.

[19] The Dialogue book series, published by Bobbs-Merrill, provides one example of this possibility.

relating to one another on the basis of problems has been stimulated somewhat by television. Having watched the civil rights struggle and the war in Vietnam on their television sets, clergy have broken the bounds of local hierarchical patterns and joined hands in concern.

The most visible breakthrough, however, will occur when electronic technology takes over in the field of architecture and regional planning. Let me predict that within ten years the majority of new building will be done with compatible prefabricated components, which can be assembled in many forms, taken apart, and assembled in new forms without loss. With the aid of computers, everyone will be able to participate in the ongoing design of his own community.

4. HOW TO SURVIVE

The advent of electronic technology represents a major change in the environment of man, even if it is a man-made change. Organisms that cannot adapt (when there is a major change in their environment) become extinct. In our case, the danger is that we will not decentralize fast enough or thoroughly enough. At the present time, electronic technology is being used primarily to generate an idiotic consensus, to wash over such nasty little problems as the imminent degeneration of planet earth. What is a proper way to treat the dying dinosaurs so that they do not chew up the entire world and take it with them?

A substantial number of people learning to live (and living to learn) in the electronic age seem to do the following:

(a.) *Drop out.* They gradually stop feeding themselves to the dinosaurs. People (who are earning a living, doing things they do not want to do, responding to positive and negative sanctions, being educated, etc.) simply begin to phase out their relationship with authority.

(b.) *Tune in.* Through a variety of methods including

meditation, they develop awareness of themselves as total human beings in a total environment.

(c.) *Plug in.* They form communities of purpose. They engage in dialogue with persons whose experience and understanding supports their own and with persons whose experience and understanding challenges their own.

In the refined atmosphere at the very top of dinosaurs are the directors of contemporary world society who don't like to think about what's happening. The only way they seem capable of entering any age is to stumble in backward, retreating on emaciated dinosaurs. If some of these gentlemen care to enter the electronic age with a little dignity, they had best climb down and attempt to mingle with their species. The world is sick and tired of dinosaur dances directed by self-appointed emissaries of God.

"God" has become a three-letter word, and no longer a sacred one. Heretofore, the word "God" invoked Authority. But Authority is dead. In the future, if we use the word "God" in any serious way at all, we shall probably use it as a signal that says, "All right, now let's sit down and explore the long-term implications of these technological developments. How will they affect our life style? What roles do we play in God? How will God play in us?" "God" will be a label for what's happening in Universe, and where it's at.

Never again will it be possible to have order among human beings by invoking authority. One will have to invoke purposes, and insofar as people care to participate in purposes there will be order. Most of the jobs and other authority-sanctioned positions that exist today have no intrinsic value: they exist not for any creative purpose but so that people can stake a claim on creation. They are absurd.

An economic-security program, short-circuiting the sanctions of authority as it would, makes a great deal of sense. It would represent a clear mandate for learning. People will enter the age of learning when they see that it is necessary. With some preparatory organization, an economic security program would release an immediate surge of creative activity, engulfing the globe. Without preparation, many people would become even more bewildered than they are today. But they would get over it.

The main thing is we had best enter the age of learning without delay and extend opportunities for use of electronic-age methods to as many persons as possible. The majority of African persons, being not far removed from tribal life, could easily make splendid use of these opportunities, advancing very rapidly while avoiding the bloody military confrontations that lie in their present path. Other groups, being more or less tied into rigid socioeconomic structures, will have greater difficulty since they (Germans, Indians, Latin Americans, etc.) will have to acquire a whole new world view, whereas Africans will only have to acquire new technical skills.

If electronic-age methods do not become the primary methods for coordinating human life on earth within ten years, we shall probably have passed the point of being able to save ourselves. Those still living on earth (if any) would have to be evacuated by empathic beings from other regions of Universe and nursed back to health.

We had best not count on the latter possibility. And we had best not throw up our arms in despair. More than half the world's population is under twenty-five. Less than one-fifth of the world's population has a vested interest in the mechanical age. Less than 1 per cent is genuinely committed to the mechanical age. Moreover, the technological environment will increasingly favor those who seek to foster the artistic development of man on earth. The actions of empire builders will look increasingly absurd against the backdrop of Universe. There is ground for enthusiasm in facing the challenge of this new age.

THE CHALLENGE OF ECONOMIC SECURITY TO RELIGION

Henry Malcolm

"Non-repressive order is essentially an order of abundance: the necessary constraint is brought about by 'superfluity' rather than need. Only an order of abundance is compatible with freedom. At this point, the idealistic and the materialistic critiques of culture meet."

—H. Marcuse, EROS AND CIVILIZATION

Ever since the dawn of the twentieth century, European and American intellectuals have been waging a war upon the religious heritage of Western civilization for the purpose of separating "myth" from reality. The attempt has been formidable and effective. No other culture, it would seem, has ever withstood such a persistent and lasting criticism without having deteriorated and crumbled. But somehow Western civilization seems to have thrived throughout the process.

What is it within Western civilization, within its culture and religious heritage, that enabled it to survive this attack? The answers, I believe, are to be found within the nature of that same religious tradition, which proves to be one of the most remarkable heritages known to man. Many religions have set the limits of reality for their faith by identifying reality with the so-called "laws" of nature. In primitive societies, whatever constitutes religious truth also constitutes political, social, cultural, and ethical truth as well. The ancient religions of "animism" are the classic examples of this unified world view.

On a higher intellectual level, much of the same phenomenon is characteristic of the religions of Hinduism, Confucianism, Taoism, and Brahmanism. In all of these famous Eastern faiths, in spite of their obvious differences, one common assumption has been shared by them all. Simply worded, that assumption is as follows: The laws of heaven (Spirit, Mind, Ancestry, or simple tradition) have completely determined the given boundaries of nature and reality. The slightest alteration in those laws has always met with considerable resistance. And the meaning of "faithfulness" to millions of believers has always consistently referred to radical obedience to these laws and their boundaries.

The Judeo-Christian tradition, however, presents us with a remarkably different set of assumptions. Although the roots of both the Jewish and Christian religions can be found firmly buried in other Middle-Eastern religions, and although many parallels can be found between certain teachings of both faiths and their ancient "sister-cults," the Judeo-Christian heritage has developed new beliefs and assumptions.

Three of the assumptions, which have now fully emerged, are recognized today as having played a most important role in the development of what we call Western civilization. Briefly, the three notions can be summarized as follows. First, all reality is historical and therefore subject to the inevitability of change. The world was created by God and set in motion on a course toward a destiny in the future, to be realized by the actual "advent" of God Himself. Second, God is not a part of the created order. He is Holy and separated from the natural realm. He may, and often does, enter history to act and speak, but God Himself is Eternal and not historical. Consequently, there can be no *sacred* places within the natural realm that possess the Presence of the Divine in their natural state. Finally, all history is determined by the "last days" (eschatology) when God Himself shall judge his creation and ultimately set things straight.

Christianity has almost always been more involved in "creating" history than seeking to preserve the remnant of faithful people. The Christian, as distinct from the Jew, has constantly felt the command to "go into all the world . . ." taking his faith and using it to convert others, to change people. Ironically, no matter how deeply involved the Church became in any given culture, there could always be found some part of the Church that was committed to venturing out into the unknown. Not unlike the Jew, however, the Christian has always understood history in terms of God's final victory over the world. The prayer of the Church, "Thy Kingdom come, Thy will be done . . . on earth, as it is in heaven," continually placed the Church in a position of openness to the future. Like Judaism, the established Church often resisted this notion, but history itself only reaffirmed the wisdom of the prayer.

The critics of religion may have cut away the mythical and magical elements of faith, but the process of technological change has done something far more drastic. It has all but completely altered the environment of the believer and the non-believer alike, replacing "spiritual" reality with "secular" fact. If God had been a "God of history" to the faithful in the past, not to be found in the created order of things, then one had to ask, "what was bringing about all of this rapid innovation?" Something has been changing things awfully fast. And to the observer of all this innovation, the only possible answer becomes "man" himself.

So subtle has been this process of change, inducing an equally subtle transformation of faith, that one hardly notices how the content of the traditional faith has now become "demythologized"; the form has remained but the content has altered. Although the words of the Creeds and the prayers of the Church remained untouched for the most part, one cannot assume that the faith of the believer has gone unaffected. God has been removed from numerous areas of faith by a large majority of believers. But most importantly, in the context of these three basic assumptions mentioned above, the process of demythologizing has been all but complete. Faith in historical change is still there, but it has little to do with God. Instead of an Eternal God who often intervenes in the affairs of men, the whole of creation has become man's secular dominion. And in the place of an eschatology that once announced the final reign of God in the last days, the search for "ends" has all but completely dominated technological man's life.

In other words, so important have these three traditional assumptions been to Western civilization that they have tended to become "a priori" judgments for the man who now lives in the age of technology. No matter how important their "theological" content has been in the past, obviously it has become expendable. But not the framework of the assumptions themselves. Without that, the technological age would be inconceivable. In fact, it is that particular framework that is the most basic tool Western man possesses in his ever-growing need to control his technology in particular, and his society in general.

In effect, therefore, the Judeo-Christian tradition has had a kind of triumph, which far exceeds the aspirations of even the most ardent believer of yesterday, even if it also exceeds the awareness of many of us today. But as a triumph, the question now arises, "are we prepared to accept such a victory?" What are its implications for us now?

Were all this no more than an issue of theological disputation seeking to establish an unverified religious belief, perhaps the matter would be open to debate. But twentieth-century Western man has carried the matter far beyond simple argument. His claim to history is irreversible. In fact, the speed by which he has been able to convert his beliefs into action has so fantastically escalated the process of innovation that any argument pertaining to the fact of change must be in terms of "how fast?"

Speed has become the one factor that has finally altered the nature of history itself. As Irving E. Kaplan shows in his essay, the speed of innovation and invention has turned history into "an exponential curve." Another way of saying the same thing would be to claim that "the future has now become a part of man's perception of present reality." Logically, this appears to make no sense. But when one understands that men who have been trained for centuries to accept the future as a distant and safe "unknown" quantity, now experience future possibilities breaking into present reality, one must then also appreciate the fact that this experience fundamentally alters one's perception of reality. Unfortunately, this is the one result the Judeo-Christian tradition never anticipated. It is not some "otherworldly" or transcendent "Kingdom of God" that looms upon the horizon about to break into our lives. It is the future itself, factual human history, filled with all the fantastic consequences of human intervention, that even now intrudes into our existence.

"ECONOMIC SECURITY: A KIND OF REALIZED ESCHATOLOGY"

In addressing himself to the issues that now confront our modern technological society, the religious man cannot escape the fact that it is his own theological heritage that is partly responsible for many of these issues. His task is learning how to accept the responsibility for that heritage and how to speak meaningfully and effectively to a world his ancestors helped create. In other words, he must now live with the consequences of centuries of belief, realized today as he could have never anticipated in the past.

Obviously, Western religions have not converted the world for Judaism or Christianity. But they have forced large segments of the world to accept new ideological ground rules; these have made it possible for Marxists, materialists, scientists, and technicians alike to share a common attitude toward history, change, secularity, and "ends." A man of faith and religious convictions simply cannot afford to leave the consequences of history to the technicians. He must join them. For him not to do so would be like the runner who set the pace for the race, and then decided to stop because victory was never one of his dreams.

And yet, that is where many religious people in the West have created an enormous problem for themselves. They have forgotten that their dream is rooted in history itself. Centuries of waiting and hope have seemed to make the dream of faith appear unreal. This is the very reason why countless believers have accepted a world view wherein faith is utterly unrelated to reality. Like the medieval theologians, they argue about the distinction between faith and reason, not simply as a point of philosophical debate, but as a radical distinction between their hopes and aspirations and the real world they live in.

Historically, it is understandable why such a separation between faith and fact took place. Everything seemed to contradict the aspirations of hope. In modern history, faith has constantly played the role of an untrained midwife in a modern highly advanced hospital. For with no more lands for Western man to conquer, the world of the believers' vision has gotten smaller. Consequently the Church has rapidly turned inward. The missionaries have been turned into "physicians of the soul," and "peace of mind" has replaced the courage of belief. Instead of the Church expanding, it is contracting. And the last frontiers are in "civil rights," poverty, social justice, peace, and a theology of adaptation to the technical world. In other words, the world is rapidly becoming a neighborhood. The world has made it almost impossible to distinguish who is really in the Church and who is not. And most fantastic of all, the ancient message concerning the dawning Kingdom of God has suddenly become a concrete viability. But centuries of waiting have made it all but unrecognizable.

Obviously, such a statement deserves explanation. What exactly is meant by the phrase, the "Kingdom of God?" The ancient understanding of the Kingdom, theologically, sociologically, politically, and psychologically has never been clear to many believers. How much is intended to refer to something totally "otherworldly?" How much of it was believed to be concrete history within the range of human possibility? And how far can we go in "demythologizing" the content of such an apocalyptic vision as the "Kingdom of God on earth"?

The "Kingdom of God on earth" is not simply an apocalyptic vision that speaks only to the "wish-fulfilling" fantasy life of the believer. It most definitely speaks to his historical existence as well. It is a part of his historical perception. And when any part of that history begins to become "real" and factual, he must recognize it for what it is. When the hungry are fed or the naked clothed, or the poor receive the benefits of economic security, the "Kingdom of God" is breaking in upon us.

In spite of the general public opinion on the subject, Jesus understood the imminent Kingdom of God in much this way. The most basic earthly hopes of mankind were the stuff of which the Kingdom was made. "Blessed are they that hunger . . . for they shall be filled." "Blessed are the poor, for theirs is the Kingdom of God." The suffering, the peacemakers, the weak, and the poor . . . all of these were actually to experience the realization of their fondest hopes. But Jesus and the prophets hardly had cybernetics and technology in mind when they spoke of the fulfilled hopes of God's faithful people. Even when Jesus is supposed to have said to his disciples, "and greater things than these shall ye do . . ." one can hardly be so literalistic as to insist that this first century figure had in mind what the twentieth century now experiences at the hand of men. But somehow the apocalyptic vision became "unreal" to the Church. And its spiritualized meaning replaced the existential sense of urgency that was so characteristic of both Jesus and the prophets.

Perhaps the most significant aspect of the alteration of faith from the original apocalyptic hope to the development of an "interim" realism has been in the experience of historical necessity. Economic scarcity has always profoundly influenced the beliefs of mankind. It could hardly have been otherwise. This is why it is understandable that Western theology in particular, and Western religion in general, had to retranslate Jesus' radical apocalypticism to make it fit the reality of simple economic scarcity. Thus if one Gospel had Jesus speaking of the poor and the hungry, the Gospel of Matthew simply reworded the sayings to read "Blessed are the poor . . . *in spirit*. And blessed are they that hunger . . . *after righteousness.*" Consequently, an entirely different set of assumptions had to be applied to the understanding of the Gospel. The fact that the Church believed the "heavenly Lord" to be One and the same with the "earthly" Jesus, only meant that the Church remembered Jesus in terms of its resurrected Lord, and not so much in terms of its earthly Master. Consequently, whole ideas were interpreted to mean something quite different than their original intention.

Actually, it was not until the late nineteenth century that New Testament scholars began to realize just how completely the Church had covered over the apocalypticism of the historical Jesus. When Albert Schweitzer wrote his famous book *The Quest for the Historical Jesus,* he concluded in good liberal form that Jesus was too deeply buried in the apocalypticism of first century mythology for his message to be of much meaning to modern man. And biblical critics since Schweitzer have directed their attention to trying to understand the "existential" significance of Jesus' message for contemporary man.

But it is now clear that Jesus can no longer be used by the Church to justify the traditional ethics of scarcity so characteristic of historic Christianity. As one New Testament scholar has said, "the Church has missed the point for nineteen hundred years." The most important area of the Church's misreading of Jesus comes at the point wherein the Church accepted the reality of scarcity as a more definitive frame of reference for morality than the apocalyptic hope of Jesus. Instead of a morality that was geared to receive the abundance of God's dawning Kingdom, a different morality developed that sought to justify the reality of suffering and human misery.

HUMAN VALUES AND THE FUTURE

Somehow the religious man must realize, as he has never done before, that the apocalyptic message of Jesus and the prophets is very relevant to our situation today. It matters little what we mean by the phrase "Kingdom of God." Its otherworldliness simply cannot continue to force us into the position of waiting and rationalizing the present moment. We must treat the Kingdom (at least its earthly components) as utter historical possibility for our own generation. It is the "interim" ethics of two thousand years that will have to be set aside. The radical demands of Utopia are upon us right now.

But what would the consequences of such a radical faith entail? Is it not a bit farfetched to assume that people can or will respond to such Utopian and apocalyptic message? The answer to that second question is simply, "no." For there is no reason whatsoever to assume that the message itself is beyond human realization. The fact that a very large part of the ancient apocalyptic vision of Jesus and the prophets is very much within our grasp ought to prove that to us. The fact that that same vision has been "spiritualized" and pushed beyond the realm of human possibility only shows how time has made ancient "truth" no longer viable as an argument against concrete reality. However, it is absolutely necessary for us to anticipate the consequences of such a change in faith and belief. We must discover exactly where the old has become empty and unworkable, and the new has become viable and urgent. Fundamentally, I believe that there are four areas where a radical change in belief is absolutely compelling. They have to do with (1) human nature and sin; (2)

the nature of authority; (3) the problem of God; and (4) the morality of "charity."

(1) There is perhaps no notion in the whole of Western religion that has caused more misunderstanding and grief than the doctrine of "sin." And of all the great cultures that have ever attempted to define the religious questions confronting man, Western civilization alone has been preoccupied for generations by an attempt to define, not so much the religious questions, as religious man himself. It was Western civilization that produced men like Augustine, Calvin, Luther, Freud, Marx, Kierkegaard, and Sartre. And primary among their contributions have been important doctrines and ideas elaborating the nature of man himself. It was not God, or nature, or the tribe that defined man's existence in Western culture, it was man himself. And almost without exception, these doctrines have described a pathological figure of utter despair.

In recent years, this Western proclivity toward defining man in terms of sin, sickness, and despair has grown to fantastic proportions. Theologians have discovered that writers, playwrights, poets, critics, and artists in general have all but adopted a theological definition of sinful man. True, their ideas have not been couched in traditional language, but the theological bent toward pessimism has been unmistakable. In fact, it has been not until the late fifties and early sixties that a change in view has been noticed, for example in Saul Bellow, Marshall McLuhan, Camus rediscovered, the post-Beat ideas of the Beatles, the Rolling Stones, and the optimism of radical theologians like William Hamilton.

The established intellectuals in our universities, seminaries, and other institutions of learning have looked upon this growing protest against pessimism as an unfounded and naive simplification of the "human condition." To them the world still lives on the balance of terror and many of them have a firm conviction that man is basically a chaos demon in his unconscious. This is why the theology of "interim" ethics still gains an audience. It feeds man's anxiety about an uncertain future, a generation that uses drugs, a society of potential economic plenty leading to uncontrollable demands for greater erotic pleasure and a future wherein George Orwell's *1984* seems to be an inescapable destiny for all men.

Jesus, on the other hand, saw sin related to the refusal of men to accept the dawning Kingdom of God. They who wanted to save themselves in a world of scarcity, justify their own righteousness by obedience to the law (which presupposed the inevitable fact of scarcity), and escape the fact that the Kingdom was open to all men were the very ones who rejected Jesus' message. Ironically, the ethics of Jesus that have always seemed rather severe to most believers—his complete rejection of salvation by any other means than openness to God's Kingdom—must not be interpreted in terms of an ethics of scarcity, but rather in terms of the end of scarcity. His rejection of the legal contract of divorce, for example, which had been given "due to the hardness of your hearts," must be placed in the context of his attitude toward what God's Kingdom entailed. "In heaven," said Jesus, "there is neither marrying nor giving in marriage." Obviously in a Semitic culture Utopia has always been seen as a place wherein the earthly reality of sex finds its highest freedom and fulfillment. It was a culture that feared overpopulation and famine, the breakdown of the economic unit of the family, and the threat of the Oedipal rebellion that resulted in the laws of "honor thy father and mother," "thou shalt not commit adultery," and "thou shalt not steal." To Jesus such legal matters had no meaning in the Kingdom of heaven. Abundance and love would replace all that.

If we continue to presuppose that "human nature" is basically chaotic and disposed to sinful rebellion against order, that somehow greed and pathological passion will break from the dark regions of the unconscious and throw a world of potential abundance into utter ruin, then we will accept controls that will ensure absolute stability and order. Unfortunately many of those in positions of political power believe this profoundly. They claim to see "depths of evil in the hearts of all men" and they seem to feel a divine mission to contain and control the world. If the religious establishments in our society continue to reinforce these beliefs, those men will soon be able to establish controls far beyond our deepest fears. In fact, they have already begun. Ask the teen-agers in southern California, any poor Negro, or any recipient of Welfare. They know how it feels to be controlled. The time is already late, and a morality of peace and abundance must now rapidly come to the fore. The freedom of the individual to participate fully in our society and to find the fulfillment of his life's goals apart from the political, economic, and religious control mechanisms of the past must now be "constitutionally" guaranteed.

Another form of this prejudicial and overstated attitude toward human nature can be found in some rather sophisticated and influential places. It most definitely is not true, as certain figures in Washington and academia have assumed, that the underdeveloped world (and that includes the underdeveloped in this country as well) must go through an extended process of evolutionary change (not unlike our own industrial age) before it can fully appreciate the benefits of technology and abundance. Such a tyranny of Western snobbery must be checked immediately. Ironically, this is in large part why the American enterprise in Southeast Asia appears very much like a "race" war. The conflict may not really be caused by color but it most definitely *is* a conflict between two cultures who understand reality quite differently. As one Vietnamese industrialist who was educated and trained in the West said, in the February 1967 issue of the *National Geographic*,

. . . in Vietnam the family means too much. It's everything. It paralyzes us. I send a boy to Germany to become an engineer— five years! Twenty thousand dollars! He returns and his father says: "I rent four houses to Americans for plenty of money; come and live with us in Saigon." The boy goes. He tells me, "It's more important to be a good son than to be a good engineer." That's what we have to change, and we haven't much time.

How ironic that this Vietnamese industrialist should speak like an American engineer. He wants employees who will work for him, he wants a highly advanced industrial society. But is it really necessary for the future of the Vietnamese people? Industrially speaking, "yes." Technologically speaking, "no." But is it not necessary that Vietnam enter the industrial era before it can reap the benefits of Western technology? Of course not. Anyone who has observed how well these underdeveloped people have acclimated themselves to American military technology, ought to realize that it would be much easier for them with peaceful technology. Destroy the family indeed! In an age of cybernetics, such an institution of the family may well place the Vietnamese people in a far more favorable situation than Western man has had in a hundred years. Obviously this means that Western industrial work-ethics do not inevitably have to accompany Western technological benefits. Somehow we must learn that men no longer need to suffer the ethics of toil and labor to appreciate fully the rewards of man's skill and cunning over nature.

An ethics of abundance and peace, therefore, cannot possibly presuppose those notions that Western man has held regarding human nature and sin. New models must come forth, models that have psychological and philosophical evidence to reinforce man's appreciation of his ability to adapt, to acclimate himself to the newer reality of technological and economic plenty.

(2) Traditional notions and symbols of authority will have to give way to more individualistic "self-determining" patterns of self-control. Ironically, however, it seems that the one issue that troubles large numbers of "adults" in Western civilization today is the apparent decline in traditional patterns of authority. Ever since the end of the Second World War social

critics have been decrying the breakdown of the traditional family structure. Perhaps it began with the industrial age, the automobile, or education, but the increasing changes in patterns of normative authority have obviously been drastic. Not only has there been a breakdown of family structure, more importantly, the family has ceased to be the model for social symbols of meaningful authority.

When Sigmund Freud at the turn of the century pointed to the military, the state, and the Church as obvious examples of group psychology patterned after the Oedipal model of the family, he hardly had in mind the fact that this classic model would seriously decline in the decades to follow. Actually there is not an institution in Western civilization that has not undergone a serious evolutionary change with respect to the authoritative symbol of "father-son" determining the underlying psychology of social ordering. It is true of government, the military, business, industry, education, and the Church. The "father figure" of the late nineteenth and early twentieth centuries is "dead."

Young people have begun to do much more than simply question adult values and practices. They have begun to create their own culture and set it over against their elders' world view. At the same time, large numbers of adults have begun to feel serious self-doubt and even emotional impotence about their role in society, their responsibility, and their traditional capacities. They no longer speak as though they held the reins of authority with any degree of naturalness or comfortableness. They often express a profound feeling of helplessness and frustration about determining their own lives. In order to cover up these feelings of inadequacy before their children, they tend to "come on strong"; but the true message comes through to the child.

The "professional," the expert, the bureaucrat, and the company are attempting to occupy this vacuum. The institutions of modern society seem to be trying to compensate by an appeal to the so-called "responsible" feelings of young people.

Although the youngsters are controlled by rules and economic power, they are asked to act as though they appreciated these controls by showing signs of capitulation: this is supposed to reveal their readiness for adult responsibility. The young who do not capitulate are often treated as "adolescent" rebels. Consequently, children learn rapidly that adulthood has little to do with responsibility or real authority, but has much to do with "playing the game" effectively.

In the vacuum that has been created, a "new morality" is trying desperately to come into being, especially among our young people. It has serious flaws and basic inadequacies, but these are the problems of a culture trying to establish a morality, a point of view, that the older generation believes to be naive and too "childish" to be taken seriously. Nevertheless it is full of life, demands the freedom of radical individual expression (in spite of what the older generation says about the long hair and Mod fashions), and it strives vigorously to give meaning to the basic interpersonal relationships between human beings. In effect, it is a morality already geared to abundance, because it takes plenty for granted and tries to individualize and humanize it. There is no deep-rooted prejudice (racial or economic) in this new morality. One can live with the symbols of abundance or renounce them, *because* one knows that abundance is not threatened by some inevitable return to scarcity.

It is a morality aimed at making "space" for the individual in a world filled with others who have needs and demands. As Marshall McLuhan points out to us, the teen-ager riding down the street on his motorbike with a transistor radio in his ear is not someone completely inundated with too much abundance, but rather someone who has ingeniously discovered a way of having privacy in the midst of urban confusion. Adults who interpret all this as adolescent "selfishness" or naiveté do not understand or believe in the basic drive of self-determination and self-limitation that is characteristic of the human being raised in a climate of plenty. That kind of criticism grows out of a world dominated by the ethics of scarcity and forced competition. Youngsters compete naturally, but only in search of an identity. They do not have to be made to compete (as in grades, business ethics, and the "getting-ahead" values of yesterday). They want adults to provide them with "useful" information and authoritative skills in mastering the complex tasks of modern life. *They do not want or need authority for the sake of authority.* They respect skill, knowledge, style, and grace. And they increasingly detest hypocrisy, false loyalty, and "gung-ho" appeals to God, school, and country.

In the world of technology and gadgets many youngsters look naturally to the adults who will not withhold from them the information necessary for their life as "involved" participants. This is why they do not understand the "conspiracy of silence" most parents demand in the home with regard to sex, the body, and honest human emotions. A morality that engenders such avoidance of reality is the first thing they try to reject. No parent can remain meaningful to a child if he refuses to speak openly and frankly about life. And no society can long hold the attention of young people that attempts to carry that ancient practice of mutual ignorance into schools, government, and business. This is why all of the ancient uses of authority for authority's sake have begun to crumble as teaching devices. If Daddy doesn't have the answers, then maybe God doesn't either. Maybe only those who find out for themselves have the answers. Youngsters want leaders, but they want them to pass information on to them. Not hold it over their heads. As McLuhan wisely said;

As the barbarian was driven to furious restlessness by the civilized contact, collapsing into mass migration, so the teen-ager, compelled to share the life of a city that cannot accept him as an adult, collapses into "rebellion without a cause." Earlier the adolescent had been provided with a rain check (a frontier to enter). He was prepared to wait it out. But since TV, the drive to participate has ended adolescence, and every American home has its Berlin wall.

(3) Traditional doctrines of "God" will have to give way to more concrete and useful theologies of "man." In conjunction with changes in language defining "sin," "salvation," "soul," authority, conscience, and tradition, concepts having to do with individual freedom, pleasure, human fulfillment, happiness, community, and self-determination will have to come into focus. Centuries of belief about the supposed "forces" beyond human control, describing history, society, and human destiny in terms of "providence," "fate," and "mystery" will need to be replaced with an awareness of the enormous extent to which men have intervened and altered the nature of things.

Scientists in the fields of genetics simply cannot wait for lucid interpretations of past theological assumptions. Their innovations have already carried us far beyond whatever "meaning" older theological notions might have had. Computer technologists cannot be permitted to construct vast instruments of control and information maintenance unless the society is prepared to "humanize" those controls and share them with the whole society. The men who have learned how to apply the fantastically significant technique called "systems analysis" must be confronted with the terrible effectiveness they are capable of possessing. Somehow that effectiveness must be determined by values and assumptions geared to serve the ends of all human beings, and not simply those institutions that presently utilize the technique. A theology of God somehow seems utterly pointless if human beings are to use it (as has been the case in the past) to keep from turning their attention toward the human beings who are controlled, not so much by God, as by their own actions.

Similarly, in religious worship, men are going to have to appreciate the fact that worship is a viable experience for people, but only when it acts in the service of the human ego. All traditional attempts to engender feelings of guilt and shame will have to be altered to release feelings of erotic and emotional freedom and self-understanding. In psychoanalytic terms, "worship must become regression in the service of the ego." In other words, the ancient symbols of religion, the act of worship itself, and the experience of regression that usually accompany worship exercises must become "conscious" attempts to use the primitive wisdom of religion, not as a pattern for reality, but as an expression of the willing participation of modern man in the ancient mythos of his past. For too long religious worship has tended to force the individual and the community to recapitulate the history of the race with all its primitive inadequate methods of coping with reality. It has been a tool of repression and control, serving the ends of maintaining only a peculiar kind of order, usually determined to rationalize the existing social order of a particular culture. The world of expanding technology needs human beings who have a conscious and free appreciation of their genetic and psychological past, otherwise technology will become nothing more than an expansion of the cannibal recapitulating his history, only now with the weapons of technology to serve his primitive hunger.

Preoccupation with doctrines and ideas about God, has, in the past, been used as a method of determining what the ultimate authority over man was. In any typical civilization that authority was often used as a means of reinforcing the existing authority of the Church, the King, or the father. But as man's insight into himself has grown so has his appreciation of religion as the servant of man become realized. The fact that this has not been recognized by most believers reflects the lag in human development that marks our age of rapid change. But religion can be a most significant instrument for human welfare.

Of course control is still a necessary human phenomenon. But the greater the chances for human self-expression (supported by a religious frame of reference), the greater the need there is for the control mechanism which grows out of individual self-awareness. A child learns the meaning of self-control when those controls become visible instruments for the attainment of individual and community rewards. Control for all other reasons is nothing but "surplus repression." This is why religion can no longer let itself be used to support the control mechanism of society. On the contrary it must become a force that clearly spells out the definitive realities any society must accept to be called "human." And that has little to do with the use of "God-language," but it has everything to do with man himself.

(4) The ancienty morality of "charity" must now be left behind in favor of a morality of universal abundance. Those economists and social planners who assume that "charity" is tenable for the present and near future will have to learn that ethics are not systems of thought structured to justify existing economic practices or social trends. Ethics and moral assumptions are values that seek to determine desired ends and viable means. Consequently, all arguments that have sought to defend existing uses of charity must be finally called into question.

For example, many of the arguments that reject the proposed Guaranteed Annual Income as economically unrealistic will have to be corrected in order that it may be understood once and for all that the GAI is a moral and ethical demand, and not a warmed-over socialist theory of economics that tries to rationalize existing economic and social ideas. It is a call for the restructuring of the present system of national priorities, an ethical demand that we move beyond the past notions of "welfare" controls of poverty, an old-fashioned work-oriented morality, guilt-motivated charity (which is a way of controlling the poor), economics that perpetuate the "myth" of inevitable scarcity.

In a time when literally millions of human beings are starving to death around the world, charity has little or no meaning at all. The nations of the West simply cannot continue to assume that the control mechanism implicit in charity is not seen clearly by the human beings who receive the charity. We must begin right now to introduce those technological mechanisms that most effectively enable other cultures to maintain their ethnic and socio-religious identities, while meeting their needs of simple human existence. Nations like America have a vast potential of human resources and talents; too many people are toiling at jobs that could easily be replaced or postponed by the establishment of a guaranteed annual income. Their freedom to travel around the world in service to others poses one of the greatest challenges the American people have ever faced.

It is a matter of national priorities, of replacing "limited warfare" with human beings who want to help other human beings; of substituting an aggressive American attack upon poverty instead of a mythological "national defense" in a world where even the Secretary of Defense admits there is no such thing. It is a matter of enabling scientists to return their skills to advancing human welfare and not human destruction. In other words, we are now facing a crisis in values wherein survival depends upon the intelligent use of human resources for human beings instead of using human beings for the perpetuation of past political, theological, and ideological ideas.

The Salvation Army may well have been a viable symbol for American charity in the industrial age of fifty years ago, but people who love to eat and dress well, who love comfortable homes and cars, ought to have a more intelligent attitude toward poverty. This is especially true since it is possible for the society, as a whole, to make certain that such factors of abundance be made available to all within our own society. There is no law of economics that says that it cannot happen. It is only a faulty morality that fears the extension of such abundance. It is the wrong-headed self-righteousness of insecure individuals who fear they may return to scarcity, who envision children without self-control, who see the poor as lazy dependents, that insists upon the controls of charity. But that kind of thinking is precisely the most self-destructive mentality possible. It doesn't realize that pleasure seeks greater certainty for pleasure, and that peace breeds freedom and the desire for freedom.

The challenge of economic security that now faces Western religion is enormous. But it is not outside the bounds of realization. American Judaism and Christianity are notorious for acting as though history never happened. This may well be the one factor that can serve us exceedingly well in the near future. It was America that symbolized liberation from the tyrannical past for millions in past generations. There is no reason why that same symbol cannot take on a far greater significance in the next few years when the very survival of humanity depends upon it. But it must now reflect the inextinguishable desire for economic security for all, or else it may well fade as rapidly as the vision developed.

Karl Marx was not the first to understand that economics lies at the very root of many religious and theological assumptions and practices. A very large segment of the teachings in both the Old Testament and the New Testament are derived from a profound appreciation of the most basic factors of economics, namely the relation between the resources of the earth, their distribution, and the needs of men. The language of religion has often acted as a rationalization for economic and political practices. All of the great economists of the past, from Adam Smith, Malthus, John Stuart Mill to Veblen, Marx, and John Maynard Keynes, would see present possibilities as nothing less than the fulfillment of man's oldest vision, namely the final triumph over scarcity. The morality that can herald that triumph lies deeply buried in the apocalyptic dreams of the past, but its realization, its practice, and application are up to us. The generations that follow us cannot help but condemn us if we fail to claim that victory. The call for a Guaranteed Annual Income and income maintenance is only the first light of a day that brings with it problems and promises fulfilled that our ancestors only dimly envisioned.

The problem simply stated is that Western man will either

accept the abundance he is making possible, learn the ethics that must accompany such a way of life, strive to share it with all mankind and thus humanize life for the generations to come, or he will develop and establish the techniques by which his technological means of greater abundance become means for greater control of human beings. Technology demands controls but only men can make these controls serve human beings. The religious enterprise simply cannot hope to survive unless it accepts the first alternative. History shows us that the tendency is to accept the latter. Human survival demands that history not repeat itself.

AFTERWORD:
THE LONG-RUN RESULTS OF A DESIGN FOR ECONOMIC SECURITY

Robert Theobald

As the debate on the Design for Economic Security has developed, many objections to the proposal have been advanced. Implicit answers to many criticisms have been developed in the essays in this volume, but it may be appropriate to put forward a direct response to the key objection at this point.

The fundamental present objection to any technique that confers *absolute* rights to income is that it will destroy financial incentives and that unless man is forced into activity through financial needs he will be idle. It is therefore argued that it would be fatal for any society to eliminate the financial factors that force people to hold jobs.

This logic is based on the psychological theorizing of B. F. Skinner, who claims to have proved, through the use of Skinner boxes and other experimental techniques, that organisms react only to positive and negative sanctions or, in more colloquial terms, the whip and the carrot. The flaw in such theorizing is that his experiments are designed so that the animal or human placed in the experimental situation has no choice but to react to the sanctions in the way the experimenter demands, for failure to do so will worsen his situation. Such experiments do prove that organisms are not *willfully* stupid but they prove nothing else. In other words, Skinner's experiments, like so many others, build the desired results into the experimental design.[1]

---

[1] A compelling science fiction story has been written around this reality. A "Skinner box" psychologist was captured by an alien race and placed in an alien Skinner box. Knowing the thinking behind the construction, he realized that he had to show that he was "creative"; he found that the design of the Skinner box made this impossible.

There is an alternative set of psychological theories, which are particularly associated with Abraham Maslow and which were clearly stated in the essay by A. A. Liveright. Maslow claims that there is a hierarchy of needs and that as a lower one is satisfied, man tends to drive for the achievement and satisfaction of a higher level. The hierarchy of needs as Maslow states them is survival, safety, belonging, recognition, achievement, and self-realization. Individuals working in other disciplines besides psychology have reached remarkably similar conclusions: that there is a drive in man toward higher possibilities. If this is true we must recognize that the policies we are presently imposing on the poor effectively ensure that they can never rise above their present conditions. By placing their very survival in doubt we prevent them from rising up the ladder of responses toward self-realization. In addition, we should be able to see that our continuing failure to help the poor clearly places our own safety in doubt and thus *directly* limits our personal possibility of rising toward self-realization.

In effect, therefore, basic reactions to proposals for guaranteed income rights depend primarily upon one's view of man. How then are we to test whether our views or the views of those who disagree with us are correct? This is far more difficult than is generally realized, for, as Gregory Bateson, the psychologist and anthropologist, has pointed out, our views are inherently self-validating. Thus if we believe that people have to be driven by positive and negative sanctions, we will act in such a way that people have to conform to the positive and negative sanctions we create. If, on the other hand, we believe that people respond to creative opportunities in their drive toward self-realization, we will act in such a way as to permit people to be motivated and moved by their creative drive toward self-realization.

This conflict in views may well result in an acute problem during the immediately needed transition from a pre-human to a human society. Most people who hold power within the present society have a dim view of mankind and act in a way that forces the powerless to react so that they confirm this view. If we are to move toward a truly human society, strategy will have to be made at two levels. First, we will have to discover what can be done to ensure that children and young people are brought up to be capable of self-realization. Second, we will have to discover what can be done to ensure that those who were educated within obsolete patterns of thought, and who no longer have the capacity fundamentally to change these patterns of thought, live out their lives with meaning and dignity.

The proposal for Committed Spending must be seen largely in the light of this latter necessity. It is now clear that the impact of cybernation will not be limited to the low-paid blue-collar worker on the assembly line. Indeed, there is considerable evidence that the computer may be more immediately effective in replacing those working on the movement of information than those employing motor skills. Thus we can anticipate very rapid attrition in the ranks of those concerned with the structured activities within accounting, architecture, banking, designing, engineering, law, management, stockbroking. People within these professions presently earn relatively high incomes, as do many of those who are being and will be displaced from the factory floor.

Would the introduction of a minimum income of say $4,000 for a family of four be sufficient to deal with the personal and social problems presented by the threat of unemployability for those with incomes near or above the average? I am convinced that such minimum levels would be inadequate because of the threat to the individual's perception of his own self-worth. Such a threat to his dignity is enhanced by several other processes that are presently developing with extreme rapidity. The middle-aged male is not only threatened by the loss of his income and by the loss of the prestige inherent in his job but also by the fact that the young are challenging his certainty of being more knowledgeable than they are and by his growing understanding that the values traditionally ascribed to males within Western society threaten to be less valuable in the future than those traditionally ascribed to females.

In effect, then, the group of middle-aged males who presently seem to dominate the decision-making structure of all the countries of the world have reached the apparent seats of power just at the time when "power" in the traditional sense is less and less relevant. We are rapidly moving away from a competitive production and transportation system to a cooperative information system. As a result the traditional levers of power are no longer effective: extreme levels of frustration seem inevitable as traditional power techniques cease to be viable. It would seem dangerously unwise to fail to decrease the tensions inherent in this situation in any possible way; we can afford to minimize the personal crises by providing an adequate standard of living because increasing the production of tangible goods and services is the least difficult task in the rich countries today.

Continuation of present income differentials for the long run would, of course, be highly undesirable. It can be anticipated, however, that they will die out, as can be seen if we trace the effect of the Design for Economic Security over time. The effects we must examine in the remainder of this essay, therefore, are not those that serve to conserve the present system but rather those that will lead to fundamental changes. We can stop examining how the Design for Economic Security will act to prevent catastrophic breakdown in the immediate future and concentrate on its potential for forward movement into a new form of socioeconomic system.

It has so far been insufficiently realized that the existence of a Design for Economic Security would not only provide resources to those who could not otherwise take care of themselves but would also provide great freedom to those with ideas about the creation of a desirable future. As George Nelson pointed out in his essay, many people who are trapped within the structures of the industrial age have important ideas about the future but do not have the time and energy to develop their creativity because they have to earn a living. The Design for Economic Security would enable such people to break out of their present activities and devote their time to working for the meaningful change they have the capacity to develop.

The most immediate consequence of this development would be a change in prestige structures. As the society will have to pay ever-more attention to social innovation and less to production and transportation, prestige will be accorded to those involved with social innovation. An increasing number of those most concerned about societal innovation will be living on the resources available from the Design for Economic Security. Receiving funds from the Design for Economic Security would therefore cease to be considered evidence of incapacity and become, instead, potentially prestigious, for many of those most valued by the society will be using resources provided by the Design.

This shift in prestige structures will eventually come to encompass all those living on resources derived from the Design for Economic Security. Such all-inclusiveness will tend to develop because a growing number of communities and consentives—groups of people working at common activities using resources derived from the Design for Economic Security—will pay less and less attention to the circulation of money within the group. There will be a tendency to find new social techniques to provide people with the goods and services they need within the group and to reserve money for outside transactions.[2]

It is this possibility and potential that explains the particular

[2] The diggers in San Francisco provide some elements of the pattern which we can expect to develop. Unfortunately, however, they in common with many other groups, seem determined to ignore the fact that it is only through the maintenance and further development of the technological system that they can obtain the freedom they want.

approach to work incentives in my original proposal for Economic Security and Committed Spending (*see* p. 196). I suggested in *Free Men and Free Markets* that we should give a person who held a conventional job or who was the owner of capital only 10 per cent more than the amount he would receive if he did not hold a job. I am now convinced that there should be no work-incentive feature at all: that we should in no way discourage the person who believes that he has enough imagination and discipline to determine what he should do to develop himself and his society.[3]

Our basic problem even today—and to an even greater extent in the future—is to develop the capacity of the individual to decide for himself what he ought to do: the time has come to face this fact squarely rather than perpetuating the present increasingly dangerous fictions. We must therefore prepare for full unemployment rather than for full employment.

This Design for Economic Security would, of course, change the pattern of supply and demand for labor. As Margaret Mead has pointed out in her essay there would be an increasing unwillingness to carry out dirty, meaningless, repetitive tasks. Those engaged in such tasks would have the possibility of withdrawing their labor unless and until the advantage through receiving wages overcame the disadvantage of holding an unpleasant job: this would lead to a rather substantial upward movement of wages at the bottom end of the scale. There would therefore be a shift in resources toward those who are relatively poor and away from those who are relatively rich. The cost of many services would consequently rise.

Such results will occur because the guaranteed income gives power to those who are presently powerless because they cannot withhold their labor. It begins to equalize the balance

---

[3] It should be noted that this pattern is also most appropriate for the unemployable—they should not be penalized for failure to find work that is not available.

of power and to move us toward a society in which the ideal of a decent day's pay for a decent day's work would not be confined to those who have been able to organize but would be available to all in the society.

This, however, is still a relatively short-run effect. The long-run impact is equally important. The existence of the guaranteed income makes it increasingly possible for people to pick and choose their activities: those activities that seem most unpleasant will rise most in price. This rise in cost will place pressure on the employer to eliminate those activities considered unpleasant through redesign of the activity or through the invention of a machine to take the place of a person. Thus the decision to introduce the guaranteed income will actually provide the market with a clearer signal about the activities for which automation should be most rapidly carried on because human beings do not wish to carry out the tasks.

A similar pattern will develop for pleasant activities. As it becomes possible for people to drop out of unpleasant jobs, they will take up the activities that appear most attractive to them. As a result it will cost less and less to get people to carry out those activities that seem pleasant to them, and it will be less and less attractive to design a machine to carry them out. In effect, therefore, the introduction of a guaranteed income makes it possible to move back to letting the cybernetic mechanism of the free market determine the relative uses of men and machines. In effect, the Design for Economic Security removes the individual from the market system and makes it possible for him to act in ways that seem good to him; the rather automatic mechanism of the market can then be used for most remaining decisions.

We cannot expect to be able to move very far in the direction of reviving market mechanisms, however, without several profound shifts in the psychological basis of our society. We have already seen that we must accept a closing of the gap between the extremes of the income spectrum.

Second, we must modify our present belief that "enough" is always more than present income: that a better way of life can always be achieved if one raises one's income. This belief, which has been sedulously fostered by economists and advertisers, is now fully contradicted by work in psychology and physiology.

In effect, the capacity of the brain and senses is limited. If one overloads the senses and the brain, a slowing down of mental and sensual activity occurs and eventually a complete blackout takes place: this can be clearly seen, for example, in the anesthesia technique used in drilling where earphones are placed on the ears and the sound level raised until it deadens pain. In effect, therefore, there is an optimum point for sensory input for each individual: satisfaction increases with increasing sensory input up to this point and decreases if sensory input moves past this point.

At the present time, it seems certain that almost all those in the mainstream of Western societies are suffering from sensory overload and that they would benefit from a decrease in their intake of sights, sounds, and messages of all sorts. There is evidence that the need to reduce sensory input is being learned by many—particularly by the young. Once this lesson has been learned, it will be understood that satisfaction is not necessarily achieved by a further increase in income but rather by a pattern of life that leads to self-realization.

In addition, we must cease to accept waste and pollution. Economists have always concentrated their attention on the favorable impact of economic growth and have reinforced their view by setting up a system in which any activity, whether it be favorable or unfavorable, is seen as adding to the Gross National Product. Thus the chemicals produced by a factory are considered part of the Gross National Product and so is the cost of the effort that later has to be made to eliminate the pollution caused by the production of the chemicals: the creation of a new building and the destruction of an old building are also both considered part of the Gross National Product.

This form of national accounting has encouraged all activities, however useless or even damaging they may be. We urgently need to examine what activities have substantial negative components and to determine how we can eliminate them. The present social concern about air and water pollution, about excessive commuting time, about the effects of tobacco are all part of the growing analysis of the dangerous side effects of economic growth. The time would therefore seem particularly propitious to develop a new form of social accounting that sees growth as a means and not an end, and that examines the impact of changes in terms of their effect on the overall ecology and the potential of each human being for the maximum realization of his own uniqueness.[4]

The proposed Design for Economic Security will permit such developments. Once we recognize that enough can be enough and that waste is intolerable, it will be within our power to provide enough food, clothing, and shelter as well as the other necessities for self-realization for each individual, both in this country and abroad. As this process continues we will come to recognize that we are indeed moving into a situation of psychological abundance and that there is no need to continue to allocate goods through money. Money is, in this context, a rationing mechanism and will be anachronistic in a society in which each person can have what he needs and no longer demands more than he needs.

Most discussions of the Design for Economic Security attack it on the grounds that it will not solve all our existing problems. This argument is irrelevant for two reasons. First, it has never been suggested that the Design for Economic

[4] One other bias in national income accounting also deserves to be mentioned. The services of housewives are not counted: thus each woman who goes out to work causes apparent income to rise although the value of her services may well be greater within the home. It is urgent that this anomaly be corrected for it causes substantial distortions in policy planning.

Security would solve *all* the problems of the society. Rather it has been argued that the Design for Economic Security is the indispensable first step to permit us to move out of the traps in which we are presently held by the industrial age system. Second, the Design for Economic Security is not— nor can any policy be—the end of the line. It is part of the continuing change within which we live. I believe that we can already perceive the possibility of a society in which the economic needs of man will be possible of fulfillment and where man will come to concentrate on what he will do because toil is no longer necessary.[5]

Such suggestions would have been dismissed as unrealistic a few years ago. Today, however, almost all those engaged in studying the impact of the new technologies agree that this is the level at which we must discuss the issues that face us. The choice we must make can be very simply stated. More economists still believe that man must toil for an unlimited period into the future; that men cannot—indeed must not—be set free to do what they believe is important because if this were to occur the business of the society would not be done. The thesis of most of the authors in this volume is precisely the opposite: that it is only insofar as we set man free to pursue his own concerns and to develop himself and his society that we can hope to live in the technological system we are so rapidly creating around ourselves.

It is for us to decide what future we can and should create.

[5] Economics has controlled our lives for too long. We can now afford to work toward a system in which goods are free and in which people choose their activities while we develop machines to do the jobs that do not interest people. Present economics is an industrial age discipline: it has become obsolete with the coming of the cybernetics era.

APPENDIX:

THE DESIGN FOR ECONOMIC SECURITY AS ORIGINALLY PUBLISHED IN *FREE MEN AND FREE MARKETS*

Robert Theobald

This book proposes the development of *new principles specifically designed to break the link between jobs and income. Implementation of these principles must necessarily be carried out by the government as the sole body concerned with every member of society and with the adequate functioning of the total socioeconomic system.* . . .

In order to ensure that government concern with the total socioeconomic system would not outweigh its responsibility to every member of society, a due-income from government should be given as an *absolute constitutional right,* for unless this is guaranteed the government would have the possibility of developing the most extreme form of tyranny imaginable. During the process of implementation of the due-income principles, the number of people obtaining the totality of their living expenses from the government would increase rapidly; if the right to these incomes could be withdrawn under *any* circumstances, government would have the power to deprive the individual not only of the pursuit of happiness but also of liberty and even, in effect, of life itself. This *absolute* right to a due-income would be essentially a new principle in jurisprudence. Most present constitutional rights can be curtailed when the overall good of society is held to require this; however, the right of an individual to a due-income could not, in itself, endanger the state.

It is clear that any attempt to break the stranglehold of the job-income link will have to be made with the interests of both the individual and society kept firmly in mind. There is now a growing awareness that in recent years the interest of the individual has been subordinated to the drives of the economy, and that this subordination is withdrawing the values of freedom and human dignity from the lives of a significant proportion of the American population. . . .

The need is clear: the principle of an *economic floor* under each individual must be established. This principle would apply equally to every member of society and carry with it no connotation of personal inadequacy or implication that an undeserved income was being received from an overgenerous government. On the contrary, the implication would clearly be one of responsibility by the total society for ensuring that no member of the society lived in a manner incompatible with the standard acceptable to his fellow men merely because he lacked purchasing power. In this respect his position as a member of society would be secure; such a principle should therefore be called *Basic Economic Security*.

Basic Economic Security can be best regarded as an extension of the present social security system to a world in which conventional job availability will steadily decline. It can reasonably be predicted, however, that Basic Economic Security alone would be insufficient to deal with all the issues raised by the coming of abundance; for not only will there be an increasingly inadequate number of market-supported jobs for those with lower levels of education and skills, but it can also be expected that many of those now engaged in middle management and similar occupations will lose their present jobs and be felt by prospective employers to have insufficient intellectual flexibility to take on new types of work. The drastic and abrupt drop in income which will follow will mean that members of this group will find themselves suddenly unable to meet the expenditure commitments already undertaken as part of their way of life, both on a day-to-day basis and incorporated in their long-term plans. In contemplating the possibility of hardship for the individuals in this group, we should not forget that their personal difficulties will have far wider implications for society as a whole. For just as individuals need the support of some form of Basic Economic Security, society needs support for its standards and a source of initiatives and drive to move it toward its goals. It is this support, these initiatives, and this drive that are supplied by this group. As an alternative to allowing the complete disruption of the way of life of this standard-supporting and societally useful group, it is necessary that a method be devised to maintain its level of incomes. A second principle should therefore be introduced, embodying the concept of the need to protect the existing middle income group against abrupt major declines in their standard of living; this principle could be called *Committed Spending*. Together the principles of *Basic Economic Security* and *Committed Spending* could be called an *Economic Security Plan*,[1] a plan designed to provide security for society as a whole and for each individual within it.

The payments to those receiving Committed Spending from the government would be related to their incomes before they became eligible for payments under Committed Spending. The continuance of higher levels of income for those entitled to Committed Spending, compared to those available under Basic Economic Security, would allow the middle income group to continue the expenditures to which they had become committed and which are vital to the short-run stability of the country. However, to avoid major differentials in entitlements, no payment under Committed Spending would exceed a given multiple of the amount available to a family of the same size under Basic Economic Security.

Any Economic Security Plan must ensure that the ordering of the level of government payments, and the bases for the levels at which they are set, do not appear arbitrary or

[1] Called Design for Economic Security in this volume.

unjust to any section of society. Such a plan should be aimed at uniting the social and economic interests of all sections of society for the common good, and should be designed to eliminate the present causes for resentment on the one hand, and opposition to necessary social change on the other.[2]

[2] Detailed information on the available techniques was set out in *Free Men and Free Markets*, R. Theobald, Doubleday & Co., 1963. Available in hardcover and paperback editions.